Autism Spectrum Disorder Assessment in Schools

Autism Spectrum Disorder Assessment in Schools serves as a guide on how to assess children for autism spectrum disorders (ASD), specifically in school settings. Dilly and Hall offer a general overview of ASD, describe ASD assessment best practices, and explain the process of identifying ASD in schools. Current research and up-to-date science are incorporated in a practitioner-friendly manner, and short case vignettes increase the accessibility of the book content and illustrate principles. As the rates of ASD reach 1/59 children, and school psychologists are increasingly expected to possess expertise in the assessment of ASD, this book serves as a must-have for school psychologists, school social workers, and other practitioners.

Laura J. Dilly, PhD, NCSP, ABPP, is a training program manager at the Marcus Autism Center at Children's Healthcare of Atlanta and an adjunct faculty member at the Emory University School of Medicine. Before joining the Marcus Autism Center, Dr. Dilly worked in public schools for a decade in roles including lead school psychologist and training coordinator. As both a certified school psychologist and a licensed psychologist, Dr. Dilly bridges the worlds of school-based and medically-based psychological services for children. She serves on the Board of Directors of the Georgia Psychological Association as the president elect.

Christine M. Hall, PhD, is co-founder of the Atlanta Children's Center for Developmental and Behavioral Health, a practice that focuses on the assessment and treatment of young children. She also is part of the Developmental Neurology Program at Children's Healthcare of Atlanta, where she conducts developmental and psychological evaluations for children with complex medical histories. Formerly, she was director of Clinical Assessment and Diagnosis at the Marcus Autism Center.

Autism Spectrum Disorder Assessment in Schools

Laura J. Dilly and
Christine M. Hall

NEW YORK AND LONDON

First published 2019
by Routledge
711 Third Avenue, New York, NY 10017

and by Routledge
2 Park Square, Milton Park, Abingdon, Oxon, OX14 4RN

Routledge is an imprint of the Taylor & Francis Group, an informa business

© 2019 Taylor & Francis

The right of Laura J. Dilly and Christine M. Hall to be identified as authors of this work has been asserted by them in accordance with sections 77 and 78 of the Copyright, Designs and Patents Act 1988.

All rights reserved. No part of this book may be reprinted or reproduced or utilised in any form or by any electronic, mechanical, or other means, now known or hereafter invented, including photocopying and recording, or in any information storage or retrieval system, without permission in writing from the publishers.

Trademark notice: Product or corporate names may be trademarks or registered trademarks, and are used only for identification and explanation without intent to infringe.

Library of Congress Cataloging-in-Publication Data
A catalog record for this title has been requested

ISBN: 9780815374350 (hbk)
ISBN: 9780815374374 (pbk)
ISBN: 9781351242455 (ebk)

Typeset in Sabon
by Swales & Willis Ltd, Exeter, Devon, UK

To steadfast school psychologists everywhere, particularly my mother, Nancy Dilly, the first school psychologist I knew.

To my partner in everything, Josh Netherton, and to Elizabeth and Penny, who continue to teach me something new every day.

Contents

Acknowledgments ix

PART I
Overview of Autism Spectrum Disorders 1

1 History and Core Characteristics of Autism Spectrum Disorders 3

 Autism Spectrum Disorders 3
 Brief History of Autism Spectrum Disorders 6
 Rates of Autism Spectrum Disorders 11
 Trajectory of ASD 12
 Postsecondary Outcomes 16

2 Etiology of Autism Spectrum Disorders 24

 Genetics and ASD 26
 Environmental Risk and Protective Factors 33

3 Early Identification of ASD within Diverse Populations 44

 Identification of ASD across Diverse Populations 45
 Bilingual Children with ASD 47
 Girls with ASD 50

4 Comorbid Conditions and Disorders 58

 Medical Conditions 58
 Intellectual Functioning 61
 Psychiatric Disorders 62
 Related Problems 67

PART II
Specific ASD Assessment Practices   75

5   Primary Components of ASD Assessments   77

      Screening for ASD 77
      Comprehensive ASD Assessment 78

6   Secondary Components of ASD Assessments   94

      Assessing Academic Skills and Psychological Processing 95
      Psychological Processing Patterns in ASD 97
      Reading 98
      Reading Comprehension 99
      Math 101
      Written Expression 103

PART III
ASD Identification in Schools   113

7   The Process of Identification of ASD in Schools   115

      Age 0–3 years ASD Identification:
        IDEA Part C Eligibility 116
      School-based ASD Identification:
        IDEA Part B Eligibility 117
      Implementation of Response to Intervention for
        Children Suspected of ASD 121
      Section 504 of the Rehabilitation Act 126

8   Sharing Assessment Results and Creating a Plan   129

      Conversations with Parents about Assessment Results 129
      Written Reports 136
      Coordinating with Multidisciplinary Staff 137
      Creating the Initial Individualized Education Program 138

      Index   147

Acknowledgments

We thank our colleagues, Tiffany Aronson, Samuel Carriba-Fernandez, Julie Cash, Sara Hoffenberg, Amy Kincheloe, Cheryl Klaiman, Ami Klin, Meena Lambda, Shana Richardson, Celine Saulnier, and Renee Ussery, for their many consultations and shared expertise that inform our work and thinking regarding children with ASD.

We are indebted to Karlene Coleman, RN, MN, CGC, AGN-BC, for reviewing and providing guidance on the information on genetics in ASD presented in Chapter 3. We are also grateful to Navreet Sidhu, MD, for providing her insights and expertise regarding epilepsy in children with ASD, presented in Chapter 5. Thank you for sharing your wealth of knowledge.

Marylyn Monteiro, PhD provided helpful suggestions related to talking with families about ASD for Chapter 8. We also appreciate her permission to reproduce her ASD triangle.

Christa Aoki, Erica Fornaris, Mylissa Fraser, and Tyler Hassenfeldt all provided valuable contributions to information on girls with ASD, bilingual children with ASD, and reading abilities for children with ASD. In addition, Jen Hammel was of great assistance in confirming historical dates important within ASD.

Thank-you to our past mentors and supervisors who have taught us both the art and the science of evaluating children and supporting their families.

Also, thank-you to the general education teachers, special education teachers, speech and language pathologists, occupational therapists, nurse practitioners, physicians, and care coordinators who have worked alongside us, shared their disciplines, and shaped our understanding of ASD.

In particular, we are grateful to the children and families who have allowed us to know them and be a part of their journeys.

Part I

Overview of Autism Spectrum Disorders

Chapter 1

History and Core Characteristics of Autism Spectrum Disorders

As the rates of children with autism spectrum disorders (ASD) have increased to 1 in 59 children in the USA, the public schools have faced an increasing charge to educate children with ASD (Baio et al., 2018). With this increase, school psychologists, speech and language pathologists, social workers, and special educators are expected to possess a high level of expertise and skill to accurately identify children with ASD and assist their families. School professionals experience unique demands in conducting ASD assessments within the context of the school culture. The school culture includes unique purposes, language, norms, regulations, and history which are distinct from other environments. Within schools, some of the contextual complexities of conducting ASD assessments involve the need to conduct assessments in order to determine eligibility for special education, the complex relationships between schools and parents of children with ASD, and state and federal legislation. Although guidelines abound for clinicians working within medical settings, conducting ASD assessments in public schools involves additional complexities and requires thoughtful adaptations and extensions of best practices.

Autism Spectrum Disorders

Social Communication

The primary characteristic of ASD is a difference in a child's social communication and interactions. Typically developing children are hard-wired to seek social input. From the first weeks of life, human voices and faces are the most interesting stimuli in the environment. These interactions are rewarding and therefore reinforced. A baby coos toward her mother, a mother smiles back, and a baby receives positive feedback, increasing directed coos. However, children with ASD show a different developmental trajectory. Although typically developing children show a natural proclivity to learn from the social world, children with ASD tend to be more drawn to interacting with the physical world (Klin et al., 2002). Typically developing children show increasingly more skill in interacting with others, interpreting the social intent of others, and engaging in shared enjoyment with others.

Early symptoms of ASD are related to children's social communication. Although language and motor milestones of children are often monitored, milestones also exist for typical children's social communication and interactions. The use of gestures and social skills are included in this domain. Typically developing children use gestures to nonverbally communicate and interact. Related to gesture use, by the age of 16 months, typically developing children exhibit around 16 gestures (First Words Project, 2017). As infants and toddlers develop, they begin to use gestures not only to obtain objects they want (e.g., reach, point) or in conventional ways (e.g., waving, blowing a kiss), but then also to describe actions (e.g., using a finger through the air to describe a spaceship taking off, pretending to put their hand on a steering wheel to drive). Socially, typically developing children begin their development during the early weeks, responding to their mothers' voices, orienting to faces during the first weeks of life, and socially returning a mother's smile (DeCasper & Fifer, 1980; Haith, Bergman, & Moore, 1977; Kaye & Fogel, 1980). These are some of the early social communication and interaction skills that children with ASD may miss or delay developing. They are often the red flags that a child may have an ASD.

As children with ASD progress through school, social communication and interactions continue to lag. They can struggle more with forming

Table 1.1 Early social and communication milestones

Age (months)	Social milestones	Communication milestones
9	Smiles and laughs at others with eye contact	Consonant vowel repetitions (e.g., mamama and babababa)
12	Plays social games like peek-a-boo and patty cake Responds to their name	Says first words (e.g., mama, uh-oh) Uses showing and giving gestures
18	Simple pretend play (e.g., feeding a baby doll) Shows affection to familiar people Imitates adults' words and actions	Uses at least 16 gestures (e.g., pointing, shaking head "No," waving, blowing a kiss) Uses more than 10 words
24	Takes interest in other children in games like chase	Speaks in short phrases (e.g., "More juice") Uses at least 50–100 words
36	Takes turns in conversation Engages in make-believe play with others Shows concern for others who are upset	Speaks in short sentences Follows two to three step directions

Table 1.2 Resources on typical development and developmental differences

Learn the Signs. Act Early (https://www.cdc.gov/ncbddd/actearly/index.html): The Center for Disease Control and Prevention's free developmental milestone tracking app, growth charts, and books.

First Words Project (http://firstwordsproject.com/): Online lookbooks and growth charts related to children's development in the areas of language, gestures, imagination, social connectedness, cooperation, and critical thinking that is supported by research at Florida State University.

Autism Navigator (http://www.autismnavigator.com/): Collection of online resources and videos for professionals and families to explore autism that was created by the Autism Institute at the Florida State University College of Medicine.

---

friendships as well as knowing how to initiate and respond to interactions with their peers appropriately. Pragmatic aspects of language such as the back and forth of conversations of interest to others and use of appropriate body language may be challenging for children with ASD. Figurative language and idioms may be also difficult to understand. Children and youth on the spectrum may also struggle in understanding and expressing emotions.

Repetitive, Restricted Patterns of Behavior and Interests

In addition to differences in social communication and interests, children with ASD also exhibit patterns of repetitive, restrictive behaviors and/or interests. One pattern of repetitive behavior that children may demonstrate is stereotypic behaviors such as hand flapping, jumping, tensing and shaking, and spinning. In addition, their language may contain echoes of statements made by others or heard in their favorite videos. They may also like spinning or lining up objects. Second, children with ASD may by highly dependent on routines or patterns of behavior. They may become very upset when a change in routine is made or have difficulty transitioning between activities in the classroom. Transitioning in from recess, going on a field trip, or having an assembly is often a trigger for problem behavior. Their thinking can be very rigid. For example, they may be described as thinking in black and white or being very particular about the use of words and language. Third, children with ASD may have an excessively strong interest in an object or topic. For example, a child may be overly focused on blue straws, trains, princesses, garbage, the Civil War, or Justin Bieber. Finally, children with ASD may demonstrate differences in how they respond to sensory input. Children may seek out visual input from lights and mirrors, sounds by putting their ear to the radio, smells by smelling objects that are not food, or touch by rubbing objects to their hand or face. In contrast, some children with ASD show adverse reactions to sensory input like loud sounds such as fire alarms, crowded events like baseball games, touch from clothing or shoes, and textures of specific foods. Sometimes they are also described as having a high pain tolerance.

Case Study 1

Alexa is a 4-year-old girl whose pediatrician had her parents call the school district to inquire about possible special needs preschool. Alexa was speaking a few words at age 18 months such as "juice," "dog," "mama," and "shoe." She then stopped saying these words and became more withdrawn. Now, in order to access things she wants, Alexa will use some occasional phrases to communicate such as "More milk" and "Go outside." While she does not point to what she wants, she will reach toward objects, go and get them to give to her mother, or put her mother's hand on them. When around other children, Alexa often keeps to herself. She tends to be very focused on objects. In particular, Alexa likes to carry beads with her and rub them across her top lip. She will also shake them in front of her eyes for prolonged periods. Alexa's mother states that she stomps her feet and moves her hands when she gets excited. They call it the "Alexa dance."

What social communication and interactions deficits are possibly present?

What repetitive and restricted patterns of behavior and interests are present?

What additional history regarding the possible presence of ASD symptoms would you like to gather?

Brief History of Autism Spectrum Disorders

Although descriptions of individuals with symptoms consistent with ASD in the literature have long been noted, it has not been until fairly recent decades that the medical and education communities have officially recognized ASD. Over the last 100 years, the medical system has gradually refined its diagnostic description of ASD and the educational system has gradually outlined ASD through special education law (Table 1.3). The purposes of these two systems vary as do their related laws and funding sources (Figure 1.1).

Table 1.3 Differences between the medical and educational systems

	DSM-V	Special education eligibility
Model	Medical	Educational
Classification	Disorder	Educational disability
Who created criteria	Medical and mental health professionals	Educators, mental health professionals, and federal and state legislators
Purpose of diagnosis/ eligibility	Insurance reimbursement, provide information about concerns and inform treatment	Give access to services, access federal funding, provide information about concerns, and inform educational decisions
Related privacy laws	Health Insurance Portability and Accountability Act	Family Educational Rights and Privacy Act
Who decides if child meets diagnostic/ educational criteria	Generally one professional	Law requires team including parent

Psychiatric and Medical History

The first descriptions of ASD were developed by psychiatrists in order to describe a cluster of symptoms in their patients. In 1911, Eugen Bleuler first used the German term *autismus* (Bleuler, 1950). The term is derived from the Greek words *autos*, meaning self, and *ismos*, a suffix referring to action or state. Bleuler described *autismus* as a form of schizophrenia that was particularly severe, in which individuals lived in a world of their own and were detached from reality.

In 1938–43 in Austria, Hans Asperger began to describe symptoms of autistic psychopathy while he was a medical student in Vienna (Czech, 2018). He wrote about a group of boys who struggled to form social relationships, but had some strong language and communication skills (Asperger, 1991). They tended to be "little professors" and often had a strong interest in a highly specific topic. He viewed the condition as more of a personality trait than a developmental disability and used the term "autistic psychopathy" or "autistic personality disorder." Notably, in the past, Asperger was seen as a protector for individuals with disabilities during the World War II era. However, recent historical research has reconsidered the idea that Asperger was an opponent of Nazi race-hygiene measures. Instead, Asperger likely cooperated with the National Socialism policies related to "euthanasia" for a small number of patients who were considered "uneducable" (Czech, 2018).

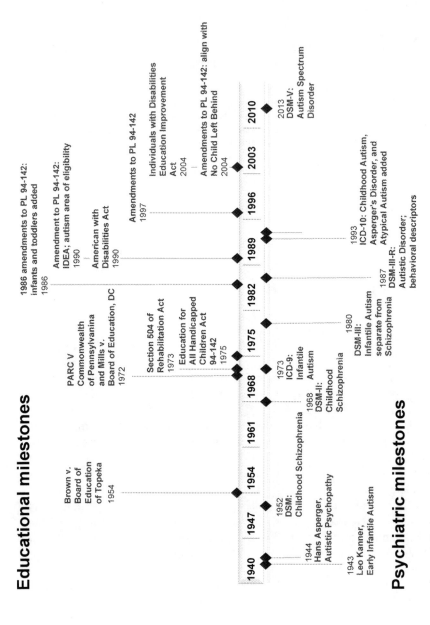

Figure 1.1 Educational and psychiatric ASD milestones

Around the same time, in 1943 in the USA, Leo Kanner described 11 of his patients as having early infantile autism (Kanner, 1943). They demonstrated what he called "an inborn disturbance of affective contact" such that they showed characteristics of withdrawn behavior, problems with change, repetitive behaviors, and echoing of language. He noted that these symptoms had been present since birth, rather than something that developed over time as in schizophrenia; therefore, he described something that resembled a developmental disability. The children he saw were more interested in the world of objects, rather than the social world of people.

More recently, it has been discovered that a third man, George Frankl, may help explain how ASD could be simultaneously described in Austria by Asperger and the USA by Kanner (Robison, 2017). Frankl had been a mentor to Asperger in Austria. He left Austria in 1937 for Johns Hopkins in Maryland, meeting up with his wife as well as fleeing the Nazi. He then worked with Kanner.

The first edition of the *Diagnostic and Statistical Manual* (DSM) included descriptions of what is now recognized as ASD under the diagnosis of Childhood Schizophrenia (APA, 1952). This continued until the third edition of the DSM created the diagnosis of Infantile Autism, separating it from Schizophrenia (APA, 1980). The DSM-III-R created the diagnosis of Autistic Disorder and provided the first behavioral descriptions of autism (APA, 1987).

Then, in 1994, the DSM-IV added diagnoses of Asperger's Syndrome and Pervasive Developmental Disorder, Not Otherwise Specified (APA, 1994). Most recently, in the DSM-V, all forms of ASD have been collapsed into the diagnosis of Autism Spectrum Disorder (APA, 2013). According to the DSM-V, individuals with ASD must show (1) persistent deficits in social communication and social interaction across multiple contexts, and (2) restricted, repetitive patterns of behavior, interests, or activities. These symptoms have to have been present since early childhood and must currently affect social, occupational, or other areas of functioning. Specifiers related to the level of support that an individual needs in the areas of social communication/interactions and restricted, repetitive behaviors and interests can also be added.

The *International Classification of Diseases* is the classification system that is most broadly, internationally used in medical settings. Within this classification system, the ICD-9 first identified ASD symptoms in 1973, using the term "infantile autism" (World Health Organization or WHO, 1973). The most current version, the ICD-10, aligns most closely with the DSM-IV criteria for Childhood Autism, Asperger's Disorder, and Atypical Autism (i.e., Pervasive Developmental Disorder – WHO, 1993).

Educational History

Although the psychiatric identification of symptoms associated with ASD started in the beginning of the twentieth century, it was not until much later in the twentieth century that developments within the realm of public education began to identify children with ASD. In 1972, two Supreme Court cases sought to increase access to public schools for children with disabilities. The US District Court for the Eastern District of Pennsylvania determined in *Pennsylvania Association for Retarded Children (PARC) v. Commonwealth of Pennsylvania* 1972 that children with intellectual disabilities were entitled to a public education. Before this time, children with intellectual disabilities were routinely not allowed to participate in public education. In the same year, the US District Court for the District of Columbia ruled in *Mills v. Board of Education, District of Columbia* 1972 that children with developmental, physical, and behavioral/emotional disabilities had to be provided a free and appropriate education. These two cases formed the basis for inclusion of children with special needs in public education services.

In 1973, Section 504 of the Rehabilitation Act provided protection against discrimination within any program or activity receiving federal financial assistance for individuals with disabilities. A disability was described broadly as a "physical or mental impairment which substantially limits one or more of such person's major life activities." Along similar lines, the American with Disabilities Act of 1990 was a civil rights law that protects against discrimination based on disability.

In 1975, the Education for All Handicapped Children, Act 94-142, provided the first federal guidelines for providing education to children with disabilities. Since then, the Act has been amended multiple times to include services that are important to children with ASD. In 1986, the act was renamed Individuals with Disabilities Education Act. At this time, special education services were also extended down to children from birth to age three years. It was not until 1990 that Autism was included as a separate area of special education eligibility. Amendments in 1994 addressed discipline issues for children in special education, encouraged inclusion in general education classrooms, and extended the age range for children with eligibility in the area of Developmental Disabilities to age nine years. In 2004, the act was renamed Individuals with Disabilities Education Improvement Act. The language regarding Response to Intervention and No Child Left Behind Act was also addressed.

Neurodiversity Movement

Although individuals with ASD have historically been viewed from a deficits model, within the last decades there has been an increasing view that autism is a natural variation within the population representing positive neurodiversity. Although the medical model typically seeks to eliminate and ameliorate ASD, the neurodiversity movement typically seeks to celebrate the differences that individuals with ASD demonstrate (Kapp et al., 2013). Rather than using people-first language such as "child with an autism spectrum disorder," which suggests that an autism spectrum disorder is separable from the child, terms such as "autistic child" or "autist" are preferred. This highlights that the autism is a core part of whom a person is. In general, the neurodiversity movement focuses on individuals with more average cognitive abilities (Jaarsma & Welin, 2012).

Rates of Autism Spectrum Disorders

It is well documented that the number of children identified as having an ASD has increased over the past several decades within the medical and school systems (Table 1.4). There are likely several reasons for this increase. First, the awareness of ASD has increased substantially. The public is generally much more aware of ASD. Second, rather than only identifying "classic" autism, the spectrum of symptoms and functioning has been expanded with the concept of ASD. Third, the guidelines for determining if a child meets the criteria for ASD have changed over time.

Related to a medical, psychiatric diagnosis of autism, in the 1960s, it was believed that the rate of autism was about 0.4 in 1000 (Rutter, 2005). However, since then, the understanding of ASD and identification methods has greatly increased. In 2000, the Centers for Disease Control began monitoring the prevalence of ASD through the Autism

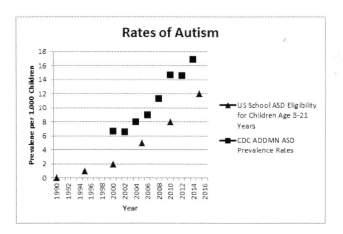

Figure 1.2 Rates of ASD

(Autism and Developmental Disabilities Monitoring Network Surveillance Year 2000 Principal Investigators, 2007; Baio et al., 2018; Christensen et al., 2016; National Center for Educational Statistics, 2012, 2017)

and Developmental Disabilities Monitoring Network. During this time, the measured prevalence rates of 8-year-old children with ASD have risen from 6.7 in 1000 in 2000 to 16.9 in 1000 in 2014 (Autism and Developmental Disabilities Monitoring Network Surveillance Year 2000 Principal Investigators, 2007; Baio et al., 2018; Christensen et al., 2016).

Within the realm of public schools and special education, children first legally began to be identified as having autism in 1995. Since then, the rate of children who qualify for special education in the area of ASD has risen from 1 in 1000 in 1995 to 12 in 1000 in 2015 (National Center for Educational Statistics, 2012, 2017) (Figure 1.2).

Trajectory of ASD

Early Symptoms

Parents and educators alike have questions about how ASD unfolds in young children and the trajectory of development for children with ASD. Although the phrase "If you have met one child with ASD, you have met one child with ASD," meaning each child with ASD is different, holds true, some helpful information about the common developmental trajectory of children with ASD is available.

During the first six months of development, children who go on to develop ASD are generally unidentifiable from their peers. Early symptoms related to decreased social engagement begin to appear after six months of age. Infants who go on to develop ASD show diminishing gaze to faces, shared smiles, and social vocalizations after about six months of age (Chawarska, Macari, & Shic, 2013; Jones & Klin, 2013; Ozonoff et al., 2010).

Although some of the earliest signs of ASD may be related to differences in how children interact with the social world, parents' first concerns are typically related to their child's language. When children begin to miss important language milestones after their first birthday, parents start to worry (Herlihy et al., 2015; Hess & Landa, 2012). Later, parents may also express concerns about their child's social functioning and behavioral difficulties.

Regression in Skills

Approximately 20–33% of children are reported to have some form of regression in their skills by their parents' report (Lord, Shulman, & DiLavore, 2004; Meilleur & Fombonne, 2009; Parr et al., 2011). This regression is often defined as a loss of language development, play skills, and/or social relatedness before the age of 3 years. This regression typically happens around the age of 1½–2 years of age. A parent might report, "Isaac was correctly using words like ball, dada, and bye-bye when he was 18 months old. Then he stopped using any words and did not use words again until he was 3 years old." Information about regression can be helpful in the diagnostic process and provide clues related to the possible presence of ASD. One caveat related to regression is that most research and information related to regression is based on a parent's report (Barbaresi, 2016). Information related to regression is rarely independently corroborated. At this time, it is not clear what mechanisms cause the reported regression in some children with ASD. We are also still learning if there are different trajectories for children with ASD who experienced regression in skills verses those that did not.

There is a specific, verified pattern of regression found in children with Rett's syndrome. Rett's syndrome affects girls, but the same genetic mutation on the *MECP2* gene can be found in boys. The mutation is significantly more debilitating in boys. Regression is a key diagnostic characteristic of girls with Rett's syndrome, and in particular, motor regression is present. Girls with Rett's syndrome also tend to demonstrate repetitive hand mannerisms at the midline such as hand wringing. Although motor regression is noticeable in Rett's syndrome, this is not a typical concern in children with ASD.

Language Development

Although many young children with ASD demonstrate language delays, this does not mean that they will always have problems with speech. There is a broad range of possible language outcomes for young children who are nonverbal at the age of two years. Some go on to develop to develop fluent speech, whereas others may continue to be nonverbal. Research indicates that as many as 70–75 percent of children who do not use phrase speech as young children go on to learn to use phrase speech or fluent speech after the preschool years (Anderson et al., 2007; Norrelgen et al., 2015; Wodka, Mathy, & Kalb, 2013). Children who have stronger nonverbal cognitive abilities and/or demonstrate more social interest and engagement are more likely to develop phrase or fluent speech. However, children with ASD who have intellectual disabilities have more difficulty learning to speak and those who have not learned to use phrase speech by the age of 10 have less likelihood of developing phrase speech in the future (Norrelgen et al., 2015; Wodka et al., 2013).

Stability of ASD and Optimal Outcomes

Children who are identified as having ASD early on in life typically continue to meet criteria for ASD throughout their life. Research indicates that about 10–20 percent of children who are identified as having ASD by an experienced clinician when they were toddlers or younger no longer meet the DSM-V criteria when they are older (Helt et al., 2008; Lord et al., 2006). This also means that some older children who were diagnosed as toddlers within the medical system may not meet school ASD eligibility criteria when they are assessed for special education.

> ### Tips for Talking with Families 1
>
> **Questions about Prognosis**
>
> One of the most common questions that parents ask after learning that their child has an ASD is some variation of the question: "Will my child be able to meet the expectations/hopes that I have for them for their life?" Parents want to know if their child will be in a regular class and regular school, go to college, have a family, and support themselves. After explaining to one family that their child had an ASD, the mother tearfully asked, "What are you telling me? Should we be saving for college or long-term care?" Families want to set their expectations.
>
> The problem that we have as professionals is that we do not have a lot of research to assist us in predicting the prognosis and outcomes for young children with ASD. It is best to acknowledge your inability to predict the future. We generally want to encourage parents to set high expectations for their children. When talking to parents of preschool children, we can let them know that some of the most important factors that are associated with more positive outcomes include (1) having functional communication by the age of five years, (2) having strong adaptive skills, (3) having average nonverbal abilities, and (4) getting an early diagnosis and intervention. These parameters, especially the two related to communication and adaptive skills, can then guide recommendation and intervention goals.

Case Study 2

Jordan is a 7th-grade student who is moving from South Carolina to your school district. The special education department has tried repeatedly to get his Individualized Education Program, eligibility report, and psychoeducational evaluation from his last school district; however, no recent records have turned up. You are asked to do a re-evaluation to re-establish his eligibility. His family reports that he previously was eligible in the area of Specific Learning Disability.

Teacher report: Jordan's teacher, Ms. Alexander, reported that Jordan generally performs well and understands concepts. His grades are sometimes negatively impacted because he does not turn in assignments. Jordan's strengths include his desire to read. He often reads comic books and likes to write for fun. However, Ms. Alexander also described Jordan as displaying poor fine motor skills when writing and doing math, difficulty with organization, and some difficulty with reading comprehension. Socially, Jordan gets along well with other students. He is respectful in class and is not easily frustrated. Other teachers reported that Jordan is cooperative and socially well adjusted. He has difficulty with written language, grammar, penmanship, and staying on-task. His strengths include his cooperative attitude. Jordan is on the swim team and enjoys his teammates.

You do have some results of an assessment from when he was in kindergarten:

> Standford–Binet IV: Verbal Reasoning – 87, Abstract/Visual Reasoning – 109, Quantitative – 126, Short-Term Memory – 94, Composite – 105.

> Beery–Buktenica Developmental Test of Visual–Motor Integration: SS = 94.

> K-SEALS: Letter and Word – 70, Numeric Skills – 83, Oral Expression – 89, and Listening Comprehension – 104.

Your intern starts conducting the evaluation. Half-way through the evaluation you conduct some live supervision. Immediately when you enter the room you notice some differences in Jordan's presentation. He seems immature for a student his age. Jordan struggles to express himself, often relying on sound effects when he had a difficult time finding a word to describe an action. He speaks very loudly with a rhythmic tone. Intonation and facial expressions are also exaggerated. Jordan talks a lot about Japanese comics and a boy in his class who causes him distress. He brings up these topics when answering questions that do not seem to directly relate. When Jordan starts to get tired he would robotically say, "Running out of energy, must recharge."

You call Jordan's mother to get more information. When you bring up that Jordan displays some characteristics of an ASD, his

(continued)

> *(continued)*
>
> mother discloses that he was diagnosed with ASD when he was two. He began receiving state early intervention services at that time. Jordan did not begin speaking until he was three years old. As a child, Jordan was very sensitive to sounds, refused to eat many foods, and did not like wearing specific clothing.
>
> History indicates that Jordan's symptoms have become less pronounced over time and that his level of functioning has greatly increased since early childhood. Jordan is currently able to function well within an inclusion classroom where support is provided in relation to his academic functioning.
>
> How would you tailor your assessment?
>
> Could Jordan be demonstrating an optimal outcome?

Postsecondary Outcomes

Although all young adults struggle to gain independence, individuals with ASD can experience particular difficulties. Young adults must work to socially engage with peers at school and work, navigate complex roles and tasks that require executive functioning skills, understand their sexuality, seek help for comorbid mental health concerns, and live independently (van Schalkwyk & Volkmar, 2017). There is also an increasing recognition that young adults with ASD are more likely to become involved with the criminal justice system. This can be because they are a victim of a crime or witness a crime, as well as sometimes becoming involved in a criminally related activity such as making a true but inappropriate comment, failing to understand unwanted sexual advances, or searching for online information that is inappropriate (van Schalkwyk & Volkmar, 2017).

As increasing numbers of children are diagnosed with ASD, the importance and success of their transition to adulthood have become critical. If correctly positioned, youth with ASD can capitalize on their strengths and neurodiversity. Within schools, formal discussions of postsecondary transitions to additional education, jobs, and living are not required until the age of 16; however, earlier conversations are needed. Individuals with ASD are at high risk of not being engaged in postsecondary education or employment following graduation from high school. Although conversations have increased about the need for neurodiversity in the world and workforce, the current picture of postsecondary education and employment of individuals with ASD is not positive.

Postsecondary Education

Postsecondary education options for students with ASD include vocational/technical schools, 2-year colleges, and 4-year colleges; however, research indicates that only about 35–40 percent of young adults who were identified as having ASD within the public schools participate in postsecondary education (Chiang et al., 2012; Shattuck et al., 2012). Approximately half of students with ASD without intellectual disabilities attend postsecondary education (Taylor, Henninger, & Mailick, 2015). Of those who attend postsecondary education, the majority attend 2-year colleges at some point (Roux et al., 2015), which may allow students with ASD to live closer to home and receive more support.

Individual, school, and family level variables contribute to whether a student continues to pursue education after high school (Chiang et al., 2012; Shattuck et al., 2012). High-schoolers who attend regular education high schools, receive strong academic grades, and have stronger cognitive abilities tend to enroll in more postsecondary education. Further, students who go on to postsecondary education have higher adaptive skills. This highlights that while schools are skilled at writing academic goals and naturally focus on academic goals within an IEP, the need to write adaptive goals and improve daily living skills is critical for students postsecondary functioning. Participation in extracurricular activities also helps predict enrollment in postsecondary education (Roux et al., 2015). These high school extracurricular activities may help prepare them for the social demands of young adult life.

Related to family and school characteristics that are associated with higher levels of postsecondary education, students who continue education following high school tend to come from higher income families as well as families with greater parental expectations that they will continue school after high school (Chiang et al., 2012; Shattuck et al., 2012). Finally, when students participate in their own IEP meeting and their IEPs note that a primary transition goal is to attend postsecondary education, they tend to achieve this goal at higher rates (Chiang et al., 2012).

Postsecondary Employment

Relatively few adults with ASD engage in full-time employment. Estimates suggest that around 50% of young adults with ASD have had a job at some point (Roux et al., 2013; Shattuck et al., 2012). Taylor et al. (2015) found that, for individuals with ASD and average cognitive abilities, 25 percent were employed; however, only 16 percent were employed for more than 10+ hours a week. In addition, the study found that maintaining employment is much more difficult than obtaining employment for individuals with ASD.

Individuals with ASD are likely to hold jobs that are entry-level jobs that have low wages (Roux et al., 2013). Jobs tend to be in the areas including office administrative work, food preparation and serving, cleaning and ground maintenance, transportation and material moving, and production and factory work.

Similar to information about postsecondary education, individual, family, and contextual level variables contribute to whether an individual with ASD obtains employment (Table 1.4). At the individual level, older individuals with ASD, those with stronger conversational skills, and those with stronger adaptive skills were more likely to be employed (Roux et al., 2013). Those with more behavioral problems struggle to obtain any form of employment (Taylor et al., 2015). Some studies have also found that it may be more difficult for women with ASD to maintain employment (Taylor et al., 2015). This may be because society has more gender stereotypes for women and more difficulty understanding social differences in women than in men. At the family level, individuals who come from families with higher incomes as well as those whose mothers have strong support networks also tend to show greater levels of employment (Chan et al., 2017; Roux et al., 2013; Taylor et al., 2015). Related to contextual factors, increased vocational rehabilitation services that support employment, living in areas with larger populations, and an early history of inclusive intervention are associated with better employment outcomes (Alverson & Yamamoto, 2018; Chan et al., 2017).

Table 1.4 Factors associated with higher rates of postsecondary education and employment

Individual	Family	Contextual
Higher cognitive ability	Higher income	Primary individual education program (IEP) transition goal associated with postsecondary education
Higher adaptive skills	Parental expectations of postsecondary education	
Stronger grades		
Participation in regular school		
Participation in extracurricular activities	Larger maternal support system	Student participation in IEP
Stronger conversational skills		Increased number of vocational rehabilitation service hours
Female		
Fewer behavioral problems		Inclusive early childhood experiences
Older age		Living in area with larger population size

Case Study 3

Manuel is a 10th grade student whom you are reevaluating. His parents explain that he had seizures as an infant. Eligibilities in the areas of Autism Spectrum Disorder and Speech and Language Impairment were established. During your evaluation, you discuss his future plans. Manuel states: "I want to be a guy with one of those bags – like the ones on TV." After some clarifying questions, you realize that Manuel is telling you he plans to be an attorney. Some of his assessment results from the 5th grade and 10th grade include the following:

Comprehensive Test of Nonverbal Intelligence-2 (5th grade): Pictorial Nonverbal Intelligence Quotient: 89; Geometric Nonverbal Intelligence Quotient: 83; Nonverbal Intelligence Quotient: 85.

Clinical Evaluation of Language Fundamentals, 5th edn (5th grade): Total SS = 65; Receptive = 75; Expression = 62.

Batería Woodcock–Muñoz–Revisada (10th grade): Letter word identification: 90; Reading comprehension: 68; Applied problems: 57.

Universal Verbal Intelligence Test-2 (10th grade): Memory: 72; Reasoning: 84; Symbolic: 81; Nonsymbolic: 75.

Bilingual Verbal Ability Test (10th grade): Bilingual Verbal Ability: 67; English Language Proficiency: 59.

Adaptive Behavior Assessment System, 3rd edn (10th grade): Teacher: Conceptual – 53; Social – 64; Practical – 65; General Adaptive Composite – 54; Parent: Conceptual – 77; Social – 71; Practical – 74; General Adaptive Composite – 65.

What recommendations would you make during the discussion of Manuel's transition plan during the IEP meeting?
How do you balance respecting Manuel's autonomy in making decisions about his future plans and demonstrating beneficence in helping him set achievable goals?
What individual level factors may affect Manuel's postsecondary educational and vocational outcomes?
What familial factors may affect Manuel's postsecondary educational and vocational outcomes?
What contextual factors may affect Manuel's postsecondary educational and vocational outcomes?

Table of Cases

Mills v. Board of Education, District of Columbia, 348 F. Supp. 866, 877–78 (D.D.C. 1972).
Pennsylvania Association for Retarded Children v. Commonwealth of Pennsylvania, 334 F. Supp. 1257 (E.D. Pa., 1972).

References

Alverson, C. Y. & Yamamoto, S. H. (2018). VR employment outcomes of individuals with Autism Spectrum Disorders: A decade in the making. *Journal of Autism and Developmental Disorders*, 48(1), 151–162. doi:10.1007/s10803-017-3308-9.
American Psychiatric Association (1952). *Diagnostic and Statistical Manual of Mental Disorders*. Washington, DC: APA.
American Psychiatric Association (1980). *Diagnostic and Statistical Manual of Mental Disorders*, 3rd edn. Washington, DC: APA.
American Psychiatric Association (1987). *Diagnostic and Statistical Manual of Mental Disorders*, 3rd edn, revised. Washington, DC: APA.
American Psychiatric Association (1994). *Diagnostic and Statistical Manual of Mental Disorders*, 4th edn. Washington, DC: APA.
American Psychiatric Association (2013). *Diagnostic and Statistical Manual of Mental Disorders*, 5th edn. Washington, DC: APA.
Anderson, D. K., Lord, C., Risi, S., DiLavore, P. S., Shulman, C., Thurm, A. et al. (2007). Patterns of growth in verbal abilities among children with autism spectrum disorder. *Journal of Consulting and Clinical Psychology*, 75(4), 594–604. doi:10.1037/0022-006X.75.4.594.
Asperger, H. (1991). "Autistic psychopathology" in childhood (U. Frith, trans.). In: U. Frith (ed.), *Autism and Asperger Syndrome* (pp. 37–92). Cambridge: Cambridge University Press.
Autism and Developmental Disabilities Monitoring Network Surveillance Year 2000 Principal Investigators (2007). Prevalence of autism spectrum disorders – Autism and Developmental Disabilities Monitoring Network, six sites, United States, 2000. *MMWR Surveillance Summary*, 56(1), 1–11.
Baio, J., Wiggins, L., Christensen, D. L., Maenner, M., Daniels, J., Warren, Z., et al. (2018). Prevalence of autism spectrum disorder among children aged 8 years – Autism and Developmental Disabilities Monitoring Network, 11 Sites, United States, 2014. *MMWR Surveillance Summary*, 67, 1–23. doi:http://dx.doi.org/10.15585/mmwr.ss6706a1.
Barbaresi, W. J. (2016). The meaning of "Regression" in children with autism spectrum disorder: Why does it matter? *Journal of Developmental and Behavioral Pediatrics*, 37(6), 506–507. doi:10.1097/DBP.0000000000000325.
Bleuler, E. (1950). *Dementia Praecox or the Group of Schizophrenias* (J. Zinkin, trans.). New York: International Universities Press.
Chan, W., Smith, L. E., Hong, J., Greenberg, J. S., Lounds Taylor, J., & Mailick, M. R. (2017). Factors associated with sustained community employment among adults with autism and co-occurring intellectual disability. *Autism*, 1362361317703760. doi:10.1177/1362361317703760.

Chawarska, K., Macari, S., & Shic, F. (2013). Decreased spontaneous attention to social scenes in 6-month-old infants later diagnosed with autism spectrum disorders. *Biological Psychiatry*, 74(3), 195–203. doi:10.1016/j.biopsych.2012.11.022.

Chiang, H. M., Cheung, Y., Hickson, L., Xiang, R., & Tsai, L. (2012). Predictive factors of participation in postsecondary education for high school leavers with autism. *Journal of Autism & Developmental Disorders*, 42(5), 685–696. doi:10.1007/s10803-011-1297-7.

Christensen, D. L., Baio, J., Van Naarden Braun, K., Bilder, D., Charles, J., Constantino, J. N., et al. (2016). Prevalence and characteristics of autism spectrum disorder among children aged 8 years – Autism and Developmental Disabilities Monitoring Network, 11 Sites, United States, 2012. *MMWR Surveillance Summary*, 65(3), 1–23. doi:10.15585/mmwr.ss6503a1.

Czech, H. (2018). Hans Asperger, National Socialism, and "race hygiene" in Nazi-era Vienna. *Molecular Autism*, 9(1), 29. doi:10.1186/s13229-018-0208-6,

DeCasper, A. J., & Fifer, W. P. (1980). Of human bonding: newborns prefer their mothers' voices. *Science*, 208(4448), 1174–1176.

First Words Project, F. S. U. (2017). 16 by 16. Retrieved from http://firstwordsproject.com/about-16by16,

Haith, M. M., Bergman, T., & Moore, M. J. (1977). Eye contact and face scanning in early infancy. *Science*, 198(4319), 853–855.

Helt, M., Kelley, E., Kinsbourne, M., Pandey, J., Boorstein, H., Herbert, M., & Fein, D. (2008). Can children with autism recover? If so, how? *Neuropsychology Review*, 18(4), 339–366. doi:10.1007/s11065-008-9075-9.

Herlihy, L., Knoch, K., Vibert, B., & Fein, D. (2015). Parents first concerns about toddlers with autism spectrum disorder: effect of sibling status. *Autism*, 19(1), 20–28. doi:10.1177/1362361313509731.

Hess, C. R., & Landa, R. J. (2012). Predictive and concurrent validity of parent concern about young children at risk for autism. *Journal of Autism and Developmental Disorders*, 42(4), 575–584. doi:10.1007/s10803-011-1282-1.

Jaarsma, P. & Welin, S. (2012). Autism as a natural human variation: Reflections on the claims of the neurodiversity movement. *Health Care Analysis*, 20(1), 20–30. doi:10.1007/s10728-011-0169-9.

Jones, W. & Klin, A. (2013). Attention to eyes is present but in decline in 2–6 month-olds later diagnosed with autism. *Nature*, 504(7480), 427–431. doi:10.1038/nature12715.

Kanner, L. (1943). Autistic disturbances of affective contact. *Nervous Child*, 2, 217–250.

Kapp, S. K., Gillespie-Lynch, K., Sherman, L. E., & Hutman, T. (2013). Deficit, difference, or both? Autism and neurodiversity. *Developmental Psychology*, 49(1), 59–71. doi:10.1037/a0028353.

Kaye, K. & Fogel, A. (1980). The temporal structure of face-to-face communication between mothers and infants. *Developmental Psychology*, 16(5), 454–464.

Klin, A., Jones, W., Schultz, R., Volkmar, F., & Cohen, D. (2002). Visual fixation patterns during viewing of naturalistic social situations as predictors of social competence in individuals with autism. *Archives of General Psychiatry*, 59(9), 809-816.

Lord, C., Risi, S., DiLavore, P. S., Shulman, C., Thurm, A., & Pickles, A. (2006). Autism from 2 to 9 years of age. *Archives of General Psychiatry*, 63(6), 694–701. doi:10.1001/archpsyc.63.6.694.

Lord, C., Shulman, C., & DiLavore, P. (2004). Regression and word loss in autistic spectrum disorders. *Journal of Child Psychology and Psychiatry and Allied Disciplines*, 45(5), 936–955. doi:10.1111/j.1469-7610.2004.t01-1-00287.x.

Meilleur, A. A. S. & Fombonne, E. (2009). Regression of language and non-language skills in pervasive developmental disorders. *Journal of Intellectual Disability Research*, 53(2), 115–124. doi:10.1111/j.1365-2788.2008.01134.x.

National Center for Educational Statistics (2012). *Children 3 to 21 years old served under Individuals with Disabilities Education Act, Part B, by type of disability: Selected years, 1976–77 through 2010–11.* Washington, DC: National Center for Educational Statistics.

National Center for Educational Statistics (2017). *Children 3 to 21 years old served under Individuals with Disabilities Education Act (IDEA), Part B, by type of disability: Selected years, 1976–77 through 2015–16.* Washington, DC: National Center for Educational Statistics.

Norrelgen, F., Fernell, E., Eriksson, M., Hedvall, Å., Persson, C., Sjölin, M., et al. (2015). Children with autism spectrum disorders who do not develop phrase speech in the preschool years. *Autism*, 19(8), 934–943. doi:10.1177/1362361314556782.

Ozonoff, S., Iosif, A.-M., Baguio, F., Cook, I. C., Hill, M. M., Hutman, T., et al. (2010). A prospective study of the emergence of early behavioral signs of autism. *Journal of the American Academy of Child and Adolescent Psychiatry*, 49(3), 256–66.

Parr, J. R., Le Couteur, A., Baird, G., Rutter, M., Pickles, A., Fombonne, E., & Bailey, A. J. (2011). Early developmental regression in autism spectrum disorder: Evidence from an international multiplex sample. *Journal of Autism & Developmental Disorders*, 41(3), 332–340. doi:10.1007/s10803-010-1055-2.

Robison, J. E. (2017). Kanner, Asperger, and Frankl: A third man at the genesis of the autism diagnosis. *Autism*, 21(7), 862–871. doi:10.1177/1362361316654283.

Roux, A. M., Shattuck, P. T., Cooper, B. P., Anderson, K. A., Wagner, M., & Narendorf, S. C. (2013). Postsecondary employment experiences among young adults with an autism spectrum disorder. *Journal of the American Academy of Child & Adolescent Psychiatry*, 52(9), 931–939. doi:10.1016/j.jaac.2013.05.019.

Roux, A. M., Shattuck, P. T., Rast, J. E., Rava, J. A., Edwards, A. D., Wei, X., et al. (2015). Characteristics of two-year college students on the autism spectrum and their support services experiences. *Autism Research & Treatment*, 391693. doi:10.1155/2015/391693.

Rutter, M. (2005). Incidence of autism spectrum disorders: changes over time and their meaning. *Acta Paediatrica*, 94(1), 2–15.

Shattuck, P. T., Narendorf, S. C., Cooper, B., Sterzing, P. R., Wagner, M., & Taylor, J. L. (2012). Postsecondary education and employment among youth with an autism spectrum disorder. *Pediatrics*, 129(6), 1042–1049. doi:10.1542/peds.2011-2864.

Taylor, J. L., Henninger, N. A., & Mailick, M. R. (2015). Longitudinal patterns of employment and postsecondary education for adults with autism and average-range IQ. *Autism*, 19(7), 785–793. doi:10.1177/1362361315585643.

van Schalkwyk, G. I. & Volkmar, F. R. (2017). Autism spectrum disorders: Challenges and opportunities for transition to adulthood. *Child Adolescent Psychiatric Clinics*, 26(2), 329–339. doi:10.1016/j.chc.2016.12.013.

Wodka, E. L., Mathy, P., & Kalb, L. (2013). Predictors of phrase and fluent speech in children with autism and severe language delay. *Pediatrics*, 131(4), e1128–e1134. doi:10.1542/peds.2012-2221.

World Health Organization (1973). *International Classification of Diseases*, 9th revision. Geneva: WHO.

World Health Organization (1993). *International Classification of Diseases*, 10th revision. Geneva: WHO.

Chapter 2

Etiology of Autism Spectrum Disorders

Understanding the causes of autism spectrum disorders (ASD) is complex. Within the field of ASD, the heterogeneity of both their presentation and etiology is increasingly recognized (Siu & Weksberg, 2017). This means that children on the autism spectrum vary in how they behave socially and behaviorally (i.e., if you have met one child on the autism spectrum, you have met one child on the autism spectrum), as well as vary in the underlying cause of their behavioral differences. For many children the exact cause of autism remains elusive and research is ongoing. It is well known that a single genetic or environmental factor does not cause all cases of ASD. Although some conditions are caused by a mutation in a single gene (e.g., Rett's and Marfan's syndromes), extra or missing whole chromosomes or smaller deletions and duplications in genes (e.g., Down's syndrome, 22q deletion syndrome), or a single environmental factor (e.g., alcohol for fetal alcohol syndrome), most cases of ASD are considered to be multifactorial, meaning that the ASD is caused by multiple factors, both genetic and/or environmental (Figure 2.1). Many times there are a variety of factors that contribute to the presentation of an ASD. It may be that a specific cluster of factors interact with each other or add together to cause the behavioral presentation of ASD symptoms.

There is increasing evidence that gene–environment interactions may contribute to the presentation of the ASD symptoms. These interactions may take place in the womb or in early child development. Genetic and environmental risks may combine to disrupt the typical developmental processes of the nervous system. It is possible that some environmental factors cause a gene to function differently. In addition, two risk factors that increase the risk for the development of ASD, one genetic and one environmental, may, in fact, be related. For example, a child may have a genetic condition that could increase the risk for ASD. At the same time, this genetic vulnerability may also increase the risk that the child could be born pre-term or need oxygen at birth, factors that we currently see as separate, environmental risk factors for ASD (Figure 2.2).

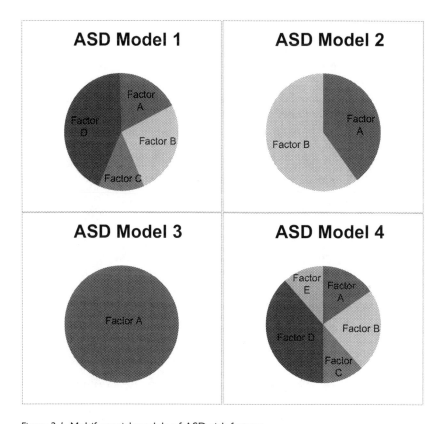

Figure 2.1 Multifactorial models of ASD risk factors

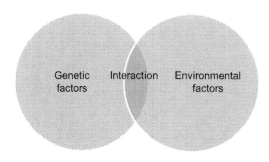

Figure 2.2 Interaction of genetic and environmental factors

Genetics and ASD

In considering possible causal factors associated with ASD, one must consider the genotype (the set of all genes possessed by an individual) and the phenotype (the measurable physical and behavioral characteristics of an individual) (Figure 2.3). It is important to understand that ASD is defined by a collection of behavioral symptoms. Children with different genetic profiles (genotypes) can be identified with the same autistic behavioral characteristics (phenotypes) (Figure 2.4). At present, the main way that ASD is diagnosed is by measurement of the behavioral symptoms. Some of these individuals will also have genetic or neurological testing or a history of exposure to environmental factors that confirms or supports the ASD diagnosis.

Genetic testing in children with ASD identifies genetic differences in approximately 30–40% of children (Schaefer & Mendelsohn, 2013). It is estimated that between 600 and 1200 genes increase the risk of ASD, including over 50 high-risk genes (De Rubeis & Buxbaum, 2015). For many children, genomic changes may be detected, but there may be unknown significance of these findings. Microarray testing reveals a deletion or duplication in 8–21% of children with ASD; however, only about 6–15% of children have a genetic difference with a clear tie to ASD (Schaefer & Mendelsohn, 2013).

Types of Genetic Testing

There are multiple types of genetic tests used in relation to ASD. A microarray is a very powerful chromosome test that is the first line of genetic testing for many birth defects and neurodevelopmental disorders. It looks at the variations in genes that make up our 16 pairs of chromosomes. A microarray is basically a computer chip with thousands of probes, which

---

Phenotype: Measurable physical and behavioral characteristics of the individual

Genotype: Set of all genes possessed by an individual

Figure 2.3 Definitions

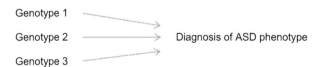

Figure 2.4 Genotype and phenotype relationships

identifies copy number variants (CNVs), including portions of the genes that are repeated (i.e., microduplications) or duplicated (i.e., microdeletions), as well as portions of genes that may have differences in the building blocks of DNA (i.e., single nucleotide polymorphisms). In addition, microarrays assess if there are identical portions of genes that are inherited from the mother and father (i.e., runs of homozygosity in the DNA). This might occur when a mother and father are closely related. The power of microarrays has increased quickly over time. About 10 years ago, microarrays contained about 60,000 probes. Currently, many microarrays contain two to three million probes.

Changes in a gene (i.e., CNV or a single nucleotide) are classified as benign, likely pathogenic, or pathogenic, meaning that the gene change is not a problem, likely causes problems, or is problematic. In addition, some changes in a gene are considered a variant of unknown significance (VUS). VUS findings are very difficult to explain to families because their clinical importance is unknown. Over time, as more children undergo genetic testing and data concerning multiple cases of the same VUS are compiled, the VUS findings will be reclassified as benign, likely pathogenic, or pathogenic. Patterns will become clinically significant in relation to patterns of functioning and possible treatments.

The next, more comprehensive type of genetic testing involves looking at even smaller portions of a child's genes and sequencing the base-pairs of the DNA. If nothing is found on a microarray, a geneticist may order whole-exome sequencing (WES) or whole-genome sequencing (WGS). Of the three billion base-pairs in the human genome, approximately 2% are in the *exomes*, the coding regions, and 98 percent are in the *introns, regions* that do not directly code for gene products. The American College of Medical Genetics predicts that, in the near future, WGS will become the standard of care. Currently, geneticists and ethicists debate whether WGS screening should be conducted on all newborns rather than the current newborn screen that looks for 50–100 mainly metabolic disorders. This would allow a family to know which, if any, genetic disorders a given newborn is at risk for over his or her entire life.

Increases in Likelihood of Genetic Differences

Children who have complex medical problems, such as seizures, or physical abnormalities, such as facial feature differences, are more likely to be identified as having a genetic risk factor for ASD (Bishop et al., 2017). It should be noted that the genes implicated in increasing risk of ASD are the same genes that can be implicated in other neurodevelopmental and psychiatric disorders. Specifically, genes associated with increased risk of ASD have been shown to be associated with increased risk of schizophrenia and intellectual disabilities (Talkowski et al., 2012).

As advances in technology are made in the study of genetics, some common genetic differences have been identified and are known to be related to ASD. Table 2.1 gives a list of genetic disorders that are associated with autism and some of the common features that you may see.

Table 2.1 Disorders associated with ASD

Disorder	Common features	Percentage of children with disorder who demonstrate ASD symptoms
Rett's syndrome (MECP2)	Affects girls; regression; loss of purposeful use of hands; wringing, squeezing, clapping, tapping of hands	50–61 (4% of females with ASD have Rett's syndrome)
Cohen's syndrome	Obesity; progressive pigmentary retinopathy	54–79
Cornelia de Lange syndrome	Excessive hair; arched eyebrows; long and thick eyelashes; flat nasal bridge; short nose; long smooth philtrum; thin lips	43–83
Tuberous sclerosis	Hypopigmented skin areas; angiofibromas (nodules) across nose and cheeks; bone lesions	36
Angelman's syndrome	Pale skin/hair; intellectual disability (ID); seizures; prominent chin	34–42
CHARGE syndrome	Colobomas; heart defects; ear anomalies and deafness; ID	15–50
Fragile X syndrome	Males: ID; speech delay; large ears; avoidance of eye contact Females are much milder: learning disability (LD); attention-deficit/ hyperactivity disorder (ADHD); premature ovarian failure	30–67 (males) Mixed sex 22–63 (1–5% of children with ASD have fragile X syndrome)
Neurofibromatosis (NF1)	Neurofibromas; café-au-lait spots	4–18
Down's syndrome	Poor tone; flat facies; up-slanted eye openings; small ears; single transverse palmar crease	16–19
Noonan's syndrome	Webbing of the neck; pulmonary stenosis; pectus excavatum (depression of breast bone)	15

Williams's syndrome	Growth retardation; wide mouth; small head; outgoing friendly personality; heart defect	12
22q11.2 deletion (DiGeorge's syndrome)	Small eye openings; bulbous tip nose; long face; dull facial expression; heart defects; ID	11–40
Phenylketonuria	Should be picked up on newborn screen and treated; untreated have fair skin and hair; ID	~5–6
Prader–Willi syndrome	Overweight; almond-shape eyes; long head compared with width and narrow face, thin upper lip and downward turned corners of mouth	19–37

(Polyak, Kubina, & Girirajan, 2015; Richards et al., 2015; Schaefer & Mendelsohn, 2013; Sui & Weksberg, 2017)

Familial and *de novo Genetic Differences*

Genetic differences in children with ASD can be of two types, namely familial and *de novo*. Familial genetic differences are those that are passed down from parents and *de novo* genetic differences are those that occur spontaneously.

For a child, his or her risk of developing ASD is about tenfold higher if a sibling has ASD or twofold higher if a first cousin has ASD (Sandin et al., 2014). Another way of saying this is that around 15–20% of siblings of children with ASD are identified as also having ASD. However, there are environmental differences that siblings experience which can change their risk of developing ASD. Therefore, even monozygotic or identical twins with approximately 100% of their genes in common do not always share a diagnosis of ASD. One recent study found that, if one identical twin is identified as having ASD, there is a 50–70% chance that the other twin will be affected (Hallmayer et al., 2011). For dizygotic or fraternal twins who share the same number of genes as siblings (i.e., 50%), there is a 30–35% likelihood that the other twin will be affected (Hallmayer et al., 2011). This is considerably higher than the rate for non-twin siblings, which emphasizes the importance of the shared prenatal environment of fraternal twins (Figure 2.5).

30 Etiology of Autism Spectrum Disorders

First cousin with ASD: 3–4% likelihood for child to have ASD
Parental-half sibling with ASD: 4–5% likelihood for child to have ASD
Sibling with ASD: 15–20% likelihood for child to have ASD
Fraternal twin with ASD: 30–35% likelihood for child to have ASD
Identical twin with ASD: 50–70% likelihood for child to have ASD

Figure 2.5 Increased familial risk of ASD
(Hallmayer et al., 2011; Sandin et al., 2014)

Tips for Working with Families 1

Evaluating Twins for Autism

Occasionally, twins need to be evaluated for an autism spectrum disorder. This can present a number of clinical and logistical challenges. Should you have different psychologists evaluate the children? Should you try to conduct them at the same time? Should you gather the history at the same time?

There are no clear answers, but it can be helpful for the same psychologist or team to evaluate all of the children. This can be particularly helpful if one twin has ASD and another does not. If two different psychologists or teams evaluate the children, the question can come up of whether there was perhaps an error or one psychologist or team is better trained than the other. If the same team works with each twin, this often means that the evaluations cannot be conducted at the same time and on the same day. Although this increases the time families have to contribute to the evaluation process, it may be beneficial when possible.

Parents can struggle to understand how one identical twin can have ASD, but the other does not. This may come from a misunderstanding that all risk associated with ASD comes from genetic factors. Reminding them that both genetic and environmental influences are involved can be helpful. Even though their children share the same genes and much of the same environment, there can be differences in their environment, starting within the womb. For example, sometimes one twin receives more nutrition than other in the womb.

There are likely unique grief reactions for parents when one "identical" twin is identified as having ASD and the other is not. Therefore, the evaluation of twins and multiples requires a thoughtful, clinical approach. Helping parents understand from the outset of evaluations that each twin will be treated as an individual is beneficial. In addition, laying the groundwork that twins can present differently despite the same genetic makeup and family background can be helpful.

De novo genetic differences are genetic variations that occur for the first time in a family. The child's parents and family do not show the genetic variation and do not have any symptoms. Estimates suggest that *de novo* mutations contribute to the risk of ASD in about 10–30 percent of cases (Sanders et al., 2012; Turner et al., 2017). This new genetic change can be present in a person's egg or sperm cell, but not in any other cells in the body. In other cases, the *de novo* genetic variation occurs in the embryo and is not inherited through the egg or sperm. It is very difficult, complicated, and often cost prohibitive for laboratories to determine exactly when a *de novo* genetic change has occurred in a family.

Dysmorphic Features

Sometimes we can identify that "something is not quite right" when we look at a child, but how do you know what features to question? It can be helpful to make comparisons and ask, "Does the child look different from other children at the same age, look different from his siblings, or look different from his parents?" It can also be helpful to see pictures of siblings, parents, and other family members if they are not present. A child would need to see a physician to formally evaluate dysmorphic features (i.e., congenital anatomical differences in a body structure), such as facial differences or other structural birth defects (Table 2.2). When present, these differences raise questions as to whether or not a genetic disorder or

Table 2.2 Dysmorphic features

- Head: small or large
- Facial profile: nasal bridge (flat vs. prominent), flat mid-face, chin development – small/large
- Bitemporal narrowing
- Hirsutism (excessive hair)
- Eyebrows: uniform, thick, medial flare
- Eyes: colobomas (a notch or missing piece in the iris), hooded eyelids, epicanthal folds (a flap of skin that covers where the upper and lower lids meet next to the nose)
- Iris: colobomas or small globes
- Mouth: clefting of the lip or palate
- Ear: rotation toward the back of the head, over-folded helix (the upper edge of the ear is thicker and folds downward), pits or tags around the front of the ear
- Nose: short, long, upturned
- Philtrum (the area between the lowest point of the nose and the upper lip): short, long, smooth
- Hands: palmar crease (especially a single crease across the palm), short fingers, long fingers. For girls: are they able to use their hands appropriately?
- Skin: café-au-lait spots (hyperpigmented areas on the skin)

"syndrome" is present. One or two minor dysmorphic features may not be significant; however, if there are multiple features, the need to point this out to the family and suggest that they consult with their pediatrician or possibly see a geneticist increases. It is important to use extreme sensitivity when pointing out dysmorphic features to a family.

> ## Tips for Working with Families 2
>
> ### Discussing Genetics and Possible Dysmorphia with Families
>
> Although genetic issues are generally outside the realm of special education eligibility, your observations may be important to a child's overall health. Just as you may cautiously recommend that a family discuss possible medical interventions for attention-deficit hyperactivity disorder, it can be helpful to point out possible dysmorphic characteristics and/or possible genetic testing.
>
> You may want to preface questions with: "I want to discuss some of my physical observations of your child, but nothing I say is meant to hurt you in any way. Would this be okay?"
>
> Possible questions to ask a family:
>
> - Have you or your pediatrician ever noted any physical differences in your child?
> - I noticed your child's ears tend to be lower set; do other families have the same profile?
> - Has your child ever been seen by a genetics doctor or had any genetic testing?
>
> You may wish to include a recommendation in your report that encourages families to share your report supporting an ASD eligibility with their pediatrician, and possibly consult with them about genetic testing and/or the need for a referral for a medical genetics evaluation. In some cases, it may be appropriate to note American College of Medical Genetics recommendations.

Genetic Testing

The current recommendation by the American College of Medical Genetics for children with ASD is a chromosomal microarray and fragile X testing for boys and a chromosomal microarray and Rett's syndrome gene sequencing for girls (Schaefer & Mendelsohn, 2013). In addition, for children with head circumferences that are at the 99th percentile, testing for *PTEN* is also recommended.

There are several reasons why genetic testing may be beneficial for families. If a specific genetic disorder is detected:

1. Families can be connected to specialty clinics and resources;
2. There may be specific guidelines for medical care;
3. The information may have implications for the siblings; and
4. Reproductive implications can be discussed.

Related to implications for medical care, some genetic disorders require screening for cardiac defects or diabetes whereas others suggest a need for monitoring of growth or preventive efforts to avoid obesity.

Environmental Risk and Protective Factors

Although genetics has indicated a strong pattern of heritability of ASD, environmental risk factors likely play an equally strong role (Sandin et al., 2014). It is estimated that up to 40–50 percent of the risk for the development of ASD is associated with environmental factors (Modabbernia, Velthorst, & Reichenberg, 2017). These environmental factors range from parental age at the time of conception, to maternal nutrition, illness during pregnancy, maternal prenatal substance exposure, birth complications, and environmental toxins. It is important to note that many children are exposed to these factors, but do not develop an ASD. Therefore, these factors are described as increasing the risk of ASD, not being a cause of it. Studying environmental factors requires close control of confounding variables because some sociodemographic factors are related to environmental factors (e.g., children in poverty are more likely to be exposed to lead-containing paint in older, poorly maintained homes). Therefore, research is still ongoing related to a number of potential environmental risk and protective factors (Table 2.3).

Parental Age at Conception

Greater maternal and paternal age is associated with a higher risk of ASD (Modabbernia et al., 2017). The risk of autism is greater in children born by mothers aged over 35 years (Sandin et al., 2012; Sandin et al., 2014). Similarly, there is an increased risk of ASD for children born to older fathers (Sandin et al., 2014). There are a number of possible explanations which may help to explain this increased risk. Maternal and paternal age is associated with a greater number of *de novo* genetic abnormalities (Kong et al., 2012). Epigenetics, which involves turning on and off the function of genes over the course of a lifetime, may also be involved. Furthermore, cumulative effects of parental exposure to environmental toxins could be at play.

Table 2.3 Current research findings related to environmental risk and protective factors associated with ASD

Level of Research Support	Factors
Research supports protective effect	Prenatal folic acid
Possible protective effective – more research needed	Fatty acid Fish oil Vitamin D
Research supports risk	Parental higher age Birth trauma Lead exposure Mercury exposure Air pollution
Possible risk factor – more research needed	Pesticides Phalates
Research unclear about risk	Selective serotonin reuptake inhibitors
Research does not support risk	Maternal smoking Reproductive technology Thimerosal Vaccinations – MMR Multiple vaccinations for young children

Pregnancy and Birth-related Factors

Most forms of reproductive technology have not been shown to increase risk of ASD when parental age, multiple births, and birth complications are controlled (Fountain et al., 2015; Kissin et al., 2015; Sandin et al., 2013b). There is some indication that there may be slight increased risk of ASD when intracytoplasmic sperm injection is used (Sandin et al., 2013a).

A mother's use of prenatal folic acid vitamins is the only known protective factor related to ASD (Kalkbrenner, Schmidt, & Penlesky, 2014; Schmidt et al., 2011; Schmidt, Lyall, & Hertz-Picciotto, 2014). Other nutritional factors such as a mother's intake of fish oil, omega-3 fatty acids, and vitamin D have some support indicating a decreased risk associated with ASD; however, more research is needed in these areas (Kalkbrenner et al., 2014; Lyall, Schmidt, & Hertz-Picciotto, 2014; Modabbernia et al., 2017; Schmidt et al., 2011).

Some maternal health and birth complications are associated with a higher risk of ASD. An uncontrolled maternal fever during pregnancy can increase the risk of ASD in a child; however, for mothers who took an over-the-counter medication to decrease their fever, the risk was eliminated (Zerbo et al., 2013). Factors such as gestational hypertension, gestational diabetes, threatened abortion, antepartum hemorrhage, prematurity, low birth weight, fetal distress, abnormal fetal presentation, and feeding difficulties have been associated with increased ASD risk (Gardener, Spiegelman, & Buka, 2011; Wang et al., 2017). At this time, it is not clear if these factors represent a clear, causal relationship to ASD or may, in fact, play a secondary role in the development of ASD. For example, it may be that an underlying problem causes both the development of ASD and low birth weight for a particular child.

Maternal and Child Environmental and Chemical Exposure

Related to environmental toxins, when pregnant mothers and very young children are exposed to higher levels of environmental pollutants and chemicals, the risk for ASD increases. These environmental chemicals can be ingested, inhaled, absorbed through the skin, injected, or transported through the placenta from mother to fetus. Pollutants can come from large plumes of pollution from factories, power plants, or waste incineration facilities. In addition, pollutants can be related to high density living such as living in close proximity to pollution from gas stations, dry cleaners, heating/cooling systems, and roadway traffic. One study found that women exposed to the highest levels of air pollutants such as diesel matter, lead, manganese, mercury, and methylene chloride were 50 percent more likely to have a child with ASD than those mothers with the lowest levels of exposure (Roberts et al., 2013). The effect of these pollutants may be stronger in the third trimester and the first year after birth, as well as for children and their mothers who live very close to a major highway (Kalkbrenner et al., 2014; Lyall et al., 2014; Schmidt et al., 2014). The effects of high levels of maternal and child exposure to chemicals such as pesticides are not clear, but data suggest that there may be an increased risk of ASD (Lyall et al., 2014; Schmidt et al., 2014). The pesticide studies conducted thus far involve children and mothers who live within a few miles of large, commercial farms.

Children's exposure to metals such as lead and mercury has also been associated with some increases in ASD (Kalkbrenner et al., 2014; Modabbernia et al., 2017). Children can be exposed to lead through leaded gasoline and lead-containing paint in older homes. Mercury exposure in children tends to occur through methylmercury exposure coming from their diets (e.g., fish). However, prenatal mercury blood levels resulting from eating fish are not associated with increased risk of ASD

Tips for Working with Families 3

Addressing Questions about Vaccinations with Families

Although many studies have found no link between vaccinations and ASD risk, families continue to ask questions about vaccinating their children. Some families choose not to vaccinate their children, increasing the risk of

(continued)

(continued)

contracting diseases such as measles for their child and other children who are vulnerable to disease (e.g., children who are too young to vaccinate, children who are undergoing some illnesses and cannot get vaccinated). These diseases are serious.

Incorrect Theories

The debate about vaccinations has largely involved three false hypotheses (Gerber & Offit, 2009):

1 **The combination of the measles–mumps–rubella vaccine causes autism.**

   Historically, the debate regarding vaccinations began in 1998 when a paper published in *The Lancet* by Andrew Wakefield, a British gastroenterologist, and colleagues described children who began showing symptoms of ASD within a month of receiving the MMR vaccine (Wakefield et al., 1998). The study was later retracted when it was discovered that 10 of the 12 patients involved in the research were suing vaccine manufacturers before starting the research study. Since then many studies with hundreds of thousands of participants conducted in many countries have not found any associations between the MMR vaccine and ASD (Madsen et al., 2002; Taylor, Swerdfeger, & Eslick, 2014).

2 **Thimerosal, a preservative in some vaccines, is toxic.**

   Thimerosal is a mercury-containing, organic compound that has been used as an antimicrobial in vaccines. It degrades to ethylmercury. This is different from the methylmercury that is found certain kinds of fish which can be toxic at high exposure levels. In 1999, out of an abundance of caution, after it was mandated that all mercury levels were to be measured in all food and drugs, the American Academy of Pediatrics (AAP) and the Public Health Service (PHS) recommended the immediate removal of mercury in all vaccines given to young children (AAP and PHS, 1999). This caused the public to assume that mercury in vaccinations was dangerous; however, the AAP and PHS action was precautionary. Since then, multiple studies have not found any associations between thimerosal and ASD (Yoshimasu et al., 2014). Even so, thimerosal is still not found in vaccinations.

3. **The combination of multiple vaccines for young children overwhelms the immune system.**

After evidence did not support the first two hypotheses linking vaccinations and autism, a third hypothesis that the number and timing of vaccinations cause ASD became more popular. However, there is no evidence to support this claim and studies have found that increased exposure to vaccines do not increase the risk of developing ASD (DeStefano, Price, & Weintraub, 2013). Parents sometimes ask about "alternative" immunization schedules; however, there is no official alternative schedule and postponing recommended immunizations leaves children vulnerable to disease for a longer period and has not been shown to have benefits.

Resources for Families

The American Academy of Pediatrics has a resource in English and Spanish for families who want to examine the evidence related to vaccinations.

Vaccine Safety: Examine the Evidence: https://www.healthychildren.org/English/safety-prevention/immunizations/Pages/Vaccine-Studies-Examine-the-Evidence.aspx

Maternal Tobacco, Alcohol, and Drug use

At this time, studies tend to indicate that maternal tobacco use is not associated with an increase in the risk of ASD (Jung et al., 2017; Kalkbrenner et al., 2012; Lee et al., 2012). However, there is some indication that a mother's exposure to secondhand smoke may increase the risk of ASD (Jung et al., 2017). A new study has indicated that, if a maternal grandmother smoked during the pregnancy of a child's mother, the grandchild may show an increased risk of ASD (Golding et al., 2017). This points to possible intergenerational effects of smoking during pregnancy which are still not fully understood. It may be that a maternal grandmother's smoking affected her daughter's egg production and future grandchildren's risk for ASD.

While it is known that drinking during pregnancy is associated with Fetal Alcohol Syndrome, there has been relatively little research considering the role of alcohol on increasing the risk of ASD. At this time, research does not indicate a clear increased risk of ASD for mothers who drink alcohol during pregnancy (Lyall et al., 2014; Schmidt et al., 2014). Similarly, there is little research that addresses potential risks associated with cocaine, methamphetamines, and opioids, although these substances are known to be associated with low birth weight, prematurity, as well as children's decreased attention and behavioral self-regulation (Ackerman, Riggins, & Black, 2010; Minnes, Lang, & Singer, 2011).

Maternal Antidepressant Use

The relationship between prenatal exposure to antidepressants and ASD is complex. The research does not provide a clear answer as to whether the use of antidepressants contributes an independent risk of development of ASD. Studies struggle to control possible confounding variables. In addition, untreated maternal stress and depression may contribute to young children's later development of ASD (Kinney et al., 2008). For example, if a depressed mother does not treat her depression/anxiety, this may decrease important early social communication with young children. In this case, maternal antidepressant medication may, in fact, be a protective factor for a child. Some research indicates a small possible increased risk for ASD when mothers take antidepressants before becoming pregnant or during pregnancy; however, a recent meta-analysis showed no increased risk (Johnson et al., 2016; Mezzacappa et al., 2017; Rai et al., 2017; Zhou et al., 2018).

Protective Environments and Intervention

Recent research has focused on attempting to change the trajectory of the development of young children who are at high risk of developing ASD after an older sibling has been identified as having it. The goal is to provide parent-led early intervention to children under the age of three who do not yet show the full diagnostic characteristics of ASD, but are at a higher risk of developing the symptoms. This research generally focuses on providing parent-led, naturalistic intervention (Schreibman et al., 2015). Supportive environments and interventions that increase the practice of social communication and interaction skills may decrease the risk of the development of ASD.

Case Study I

James is a 6-year-old boy who moves into your district. No eligibility records or psychological evaluations are available from his previous district, but your team has discovered he was in a self-contained classroom for children with intellectual disabilities. You are asked to conduct an evaluation.

James is an identical twin who was born full-term. He was in the NICU for 1½ weeks following birth. He has sickle cell anemia. He comes from an industrial city in the Midwest and has a history of eating paint chips. He had a history of chelation therapy for lead poisoning. The family disclosed that they had prior contact with the Department of Family and Human Services due to allegations of neglect. During your evaluation, you do a home visit to try to get an adaptive measure completed; conditions are poor.

Classroom observation: James was observed within the classroom. He worked with a paraprofessional on identifying letters. James' attention needed to be redirected. He was able to identify several letters. James indicated that he needed to go to the bathroom. He was allowed to go to the bathroom independently. After approximately 5 minutes, the paraprofessional went to find James. James did not comply immediately with directions to return to the class. On the way back to the classroom, a small kindergarten boy was walking down the hall. James said, "Hey" and gave the child a hug. The examiner had to prompt James to let go of the other child. James then looked in a set of mirrors in the classroom and watched himself as a he imitated what appeared to be gang hand symbols for approximately 3 minutes.

Teacher report: James shows an unusually strong interest in wrestling, rocks side to side, and also engages in repetitive mouth-clicking noises. He pretends he is a wrestler, imitating moves she assumes he has seen on TV. He has difficulty communicating with others. Socially, James struggles to coordinate eye contact with verbal and nonverbal communication. He has not successfully formed friendships; however, he shows some interest in interacting with others. He is physically aggressive toward other students, exhibits inappropriate sexual gestures, and is noncompliant with teacher directives.

Testing:

> Differential Ability Scales – II: Verbal: 56; Nonverbal Reasoning: 70; Spatial: 58.
>
> Childhood Autism Rating Scale – 2: Raw score of 33.5, falling within the mild to moderate range.
>
> Adaptive Behavior Assessment System – 3: Teacher: Conceptual: 50; Social: 55; Practical: 43; General Adaptive Composite: 41. Parent: Conceptual: 50; Social: 61; Practical: 46; General Adaptive Composite: 45.

What areas of eligibility would you consider for him? What complicating factors may be at play?

If you were to conceptualize the case as a possible ASD eligibility, what risk factors might be involved? Think from a multifactorial approach. Could there any possible environment–genetic interactions present?

References

Ackerman, J. P., Riggins, T., & Black, M. M. (2010). A review of the effects of prenatal cocaine exposure among school-aged children. *Pediatrics*, 125(3), 554–565. doi:10.1542/peds.2009-0637.

American Academy of Pediatrics and the Public Health Service (1999). Thimerosal in vaccines: a joint statement of the American Academy of Pediatrics and the Public Health Service. *MMWR Morbidity and Mortality Weekly Report*, 48(26), 563–565.

Bishop, S. L., Farmer, C., Bal, V., Robinson, E. B., Willsey, A. J., Werling, D. M., et al. (2017). Identification of developmental and behavioral markers associated with genetic abnormalities in autism spectrum disorder. *American Journal of Psychiatry*, 174(6), 576–585. doi:10.1176/appi.ajp.2017.16101115.

De Rubeis, S. & Buxbaum, J. D. (2015). Genetics and genomics of autism spectrum disorder: embracing complexity. *Human Molecular Genetics*, 24(R1), R24–R31. doi:10.1093/hmg/ddv273.

DeStefano, F., Price, C. S., & Weintraub, E. S. (2013). Increasing exposure to antibody-stimulating proteins and polysaccharides in vaccines is not associated with risk of autism. *Journal of Pediatrics*, 163(2), 561–567. doi:10.1016/j.jpeds.2013.02.001.

Fountain, C., Zhang, Y., Kissin, D. M., Schieve, L. A., Jamieson, D. J., Rice, C., & Bearman, P. (2015). Association between assisted reproductive technology conception and autism in California, 1997–2007. *American Journal of Public Health*, 105(5), 963–971. doi:10.2105/ajph.2014.302383.

Gardener, H., Spiegelman, D., & Buka, S. L. (2011). Perinatal and neonatal risk factors for autism: a comprehensive meta-analysis. *Pediatrics*, 128(2), 344–355. doi:10.1542/peds.2010-1036.

Gerber, J. S. & Offit, P. A. (2009). Vaccines and autism: a tale of shifting hypotheses. *Clinical Infectious Disease*, 48(4), 456–461. doi:10.1086/596476.

Golding, J., Ellis, G., Gregory, S., Birmingham, K., Iles-Caven, Y., Rai, D., & Pembrey, M. (2017). Grand-maternal smoking in pregnancy and grandchild's autistic traits and diagnosed autism. *Scientific Reports*, 7, 46179. doi:10.1038/srep46179.

Hallmayer, J., Cleveland, S., Torres, A., Phillips, J., Cohen, B., Torigoe, T., et al. (2011). Genetic heritability and shared environmental factors among twin pairs with autism. *Archives of General Psychiatry*, 68(11), 1095–1102. doi:10.1001/archgenpsychiatry.2011.76.

Johnson, K. C., Smith, A. K., Stowe, Z. N., Newport, D. J., & Brennan, P. A. (2016). Preschool outcomes following prenatal serotonin reuptake inhibitor exposure: differences in language and behavior, but not cognitive function. *Journal of Clinical Psychiatry*, 77(2), e176–e182. doi:10.4088/JCP.14m09348.

Jung, Y., Lee, A. M., McKee, S. A., & Picciotto, M. R. (2017). Maternal smoking and autism spectrum disorder: meta-analysis with population smoking metrics as moderators. *Scientific Reports*, 7(1), 4315. doi:10.1038/s41598-017-04413-1.

Kalkbrenner, A. E., Braun, J. M., Durkin, M. S., Maenner, M. J., Cunniff, C., Lee, L.-C., et al. (2012). Maternal smoking during pregnancy and the prevalence of autism spectrum disorders, using data from the autism and developmental disabilities monitoring network. *Environmental Health Perspectives*, 120(7), 1042–1048. doi:10.1289/ehp.1104556

Kalkbrenner, A. E., Schmidt, R. J., & Penlesky, A. C. (2014). Environmental chemical exposures and autism spectrum disorders: A review of the epidemiological evidence. *Current Problems in Pediatric and Adolescent Health Care*, 44(10), 277–318. doi:10.1016/j.cppeds.2014.06.001.

Kinney, D. K., Munir, K. M., Crowley, D. J., & Miller, A. M. (2008). Prenatal stress and risk for autism. *Neuroscience and Biobehavioral Reviews*, 32(8), 1519–1532. doi:10.1016/j.neubiorev.2008.06.004.

Kissin, D. M., Zhang, Y., Boulet, S. L., Fountain, C., Bearman, P., Schieve, L., et al. (2015). Association of assisted reproductive technology (ART) treatment and parental infertility diagnosis with autism in ART-conceived children. *Human Reproduction*, 30(2), 454–465. doi:10.1093/humrep/deu338.

Kong, A., Frigge, M. L., Masson, G., Besenbacher, S., Sulem, P., Magnusson, G., et al. (2012). Rate of de novo mutations and the importance of father's age to disease risk. *Nature*, 488(7412), 471–475. doi:10.1038/nature11396.

Lee, B. K., Gardner, R. M., Dal, H., Svensson, A., Galanti, M. R., Rai, D., et al. (2012). Brief report: maternal smoking during pregnancy and autism spectrum disorders. *Journal of Autism and Developmental Disorders*, 42(9), 2000–2005. doi:10.1007/s10803-011-1425-4

Lyall, K., Schmidt, R. J., & Hertz-Picciotto, I. (2014). Maternal lifestyle and environmental risk factors for autism spectrum disorders. *International Journal of Epidemiology*, 43(2), 443–464. doi:10.1093/ije/dyt282.

Madsen, K. M., Hviid, A., Vestergaard, M., Schendel, D., Wohlfahrt, J., Thorsen, P., et al. (2002). A population-based study of measles, mumps, and rubella vaccination and autism. *New England Journal of Medicine*, 347(19), 1477–1482.

Mezzacappa, A., Lasica, P., Gianfagna, F., Cazas, O., Hardy, P., Falissard, B., et al. (2017). Risk for autism spectrum disorders according to period of prenatal antidepressant exposure: A systematic review and meta-analysis. *Journal of the American Medical Association of Pediatrics*, 171(6), 555–563. doi:10.1001/jamapediatrics.2017.0124.

Minnes, S., Lang, A., & Singer, L. (2011). Prenatal tobacco, marijuana, stimulant, and opiate exposure: outcomes and practice implications. *Addiction Science & Clinical Practice*, 6(1), 57–70.

Modabbernia, A., Velthorst, E., & Reichenberg, A. (2017). Environmental risk factors for autism: an evidence-based review of systematic reviews and meta-analyses. *Molecular Autism*, 8, 13. doi:10.1186/s13229-017-0121-4.

Polyak, A., Kubina, R. M., & Girirajan, S. (2015). Comorbidity of intellectual disability confounds ascertainment of autism: implications for genetic diagnosis. *American Journal of Medical Genetics, Part B, Neuropsychiatric Genetics*, 168(7), 600–608. doi:10.1002/ajmg.b.32338.

Rai, D., Lee, B. K., Dalman, C., Newschaffer, C., Lewis, G., & Magnusson, C. (2017). Antidepressants during pregnancy and autism in offspring: population based cohort study. *British Medical Journal* 358, doi:10.1136/bmj.j2811.

Richards, C., Jones, C., Groves, L., Moss, J., & Oliver, C. (2015). Prevalence of autism spectrum disorder phenomenology in genetic disorders: a systematic review and meta-analysis. *The Lancet Psychiatry*, 2(10), 909–916. doi:10.1016/s2215-0366(15)00376-4.

Roberts, A. L., Lyall, K., Hart, J. E., Laden, F., Just, A. C., Bobb, J. F., et al. (2013). Perinatal air pollutant exposures and autism spectrum disorder in the children of Nurses' Health Study II participants. *Environmental Health Perspectives*, 121(8), 978–984. doi:10.1289/ehp.1206187.

Sanders, S. J., Murtha, M. T., Gupta, A. R., Murdoch, J. D., Raubeson, M. J., Willsey, A. J., et al. (2012). De novo mutations revealed by whole-exome sequencing are strongly associated with autism. *Nature*, 485(7397), 237–241. doi:10.1038/nature10945.

Sandin, S., Hultman, C. M., Kolevzon, A., Gross, R., MacCabe, J. H., & Reichenberg, A. (2012). Advancing maternal age is associated with increasing risk for autism: a review and meta-analysis. *Journal of the American Academy of Child & Adolescent Psychiatry*, 51(5).

Sandin, S., Nygren, K.-G., Iliadou, A., Hultman, C. M., & Reichenberg, A. (2013a). Autism and mental retardation among offspring born after in vitro fertilization. *JAMA*, 310(1), 75–84. doi:10.1001/jama.2013.7222.

Sandin, S., Nygren, K.-G., Iliadou, A., Hultman, C. M., & Reichenberg, A. (2013b). Autism and mental retardation among offspring born after in vitro fertilization. *Journal of the American Medical Association*, 310(1), 75–84. doi:10.1001/jama.2013.7222.

Sandin, S., Lichtenstein, P., Kuja-Halkola, R., Larsson, H., Hultman, C. M., & Reichenberg, A. (2014). The familial risk of autism. *Journal of the American Medical Association*, 311(17), 1770–1777. doi:10.1001/jama.2014.4144.

Schaefer, G. B. & Mendelsohn, N. J. (2013). Clinical genetics evaluation in identifying the etiology of autism spectrum disorders: 2013 guideline revisions. *Genetic Medicine*, 15(5), 399–407. doi:10.1038/gim.2013.32.

Schmidt, R. J., Hansen, R. L., Hartiala, J., Allayee, H., Schmidt, L. C., Tancredi, D. J., et al. (2011). Prenatal vitamins, one-carbon metabolism gene variants, and risk for autism. *Epidemiology*, 22(4), 476–485. doi:10.1097/EDE.0b013e31821d0e30

Schmidt, R. J., Lyall, K., & Hertz-Picciotto, I. (2014). Environment and autism: Current state of the science. *Cutting Edge Psychiatry Practice*, 1(4), 21–38.

Schreibman, L., Dawson, G., Stahmer, A. C., Landa, R., Rogers, S. J., McGee, G. G., et al. (2015). Naturalistic developmental behavioral interventions: Empirically validated treatments for autism spectrum disorder. *Journal of Autism and Developmental Disorder*, 45(8), 2411–2428. doi:10.1007/s10803-015-2407-8.

Siu, M. T. & Weksberg, R. (2017). Epigenetics of autism spectrum disorder. *Advances in Experimental Medicine and Biology*, 978, 63–90. doi:10.1007/978-3-319-53889-1_4.

Talkowski, M. E., Rosenfeld, Jill A., Blumenthal, I., Pillalamarri, V., Chiang, C., Heilbut, A., et al. (2012). Sequencing chromosomal abnormalities reveals neurodevelopmental loci that confer risk across diagnostic boundaries. *Cell*, 149(3), 525–537. doi:10.1016/j.cell.2012.03.028.

Taylor, L. E., Swerdfeger, A. L., & Eslick, G. D. (2014). Vaccines are not associated with autism: an evidence-based meta-analysis of case-control and cohort studies. *Vaccine*, 32(29), 3623–3629. doi:10.1016/j.vaccine.2014.04.085.

Turner, T. N., Coe, B. P., Dickel, D. E., Hoekzema, K., Nelson, B. J., Zody, M. C., et al. (2017). Genomic patterns of de novo mutation in simplex autism. *Cell*, 171(3), 710–722. doi:10.1016/j.cell.2017.08.047.

Wakefield, A. J., Murch, S. H., Anthony, A., Linnell, J., Casson, D. M., Malik, M., et al. (1998). RETRACTED: Ileal–lymphoid–nodular hyperplasia, non-specific colitis, and pervasive developmental disorder in children. *The Lancet*, 351(9103), 637–641. doi:10.1016/S0140-6736(97)11096-0.

Wang, C., Geng, H., Liu, W., & Zhang, G. (2017). Prenatal, perinatal, and postnatal factors associated with autism: A meta-analysis. *Medicine (Baltimore)*, 96(18), e6696. doi:10.1097/md.0000000000006696.

Yoshimasu, K., Kiyohara, C., Takemura, S., & Nakai, K. (2014). A meta-analysis of the evidence on the impact of prenatal and early infancy exposures to mercury on autism and attention deficit/hyperactivity disorder in the childhood. *Neurotoxicology*, 44, 121–131. doi:10.1016/j.neuro.2014.06.007.

Zerbo, O., Iosif, A.-M., Walker, C., Ozonoff, S., Hansen, R. L., & Hertz-Picciotto, I. (2013). Is maternal influenza or fever during pregnancy associated with autism or developmental delays? Results from the CHARGE (CHildhood Autism Risks from Genetics and Environment) study. *Journal of autism and developmental disorders*, 43(1), 25–33. doi:10.1007/s10803-012-1540-x.

Zhou, X., Li, Y.J., Ou, J.J., & Li, Y.M. (2018). Association between maternal antidepressant use during pregnancy and autism spectrum disorder: an updated meta-analysis. *Molecular Autism*, 9(1), 21. doi:10.1186/s13229-018-0207-7.

Chapter 3

Early Identification of ASD within Diverse Populations

Early screening and identification of ASD are critical in providing early intervention. As educators, we recognize the value of early intervention and research is indicating that it may be particularly important for children with ASD. Children are increasingly screened by pediatricians for ASD as part of early development screenings. This aids in the early identification of children with ASD. In addition, there is increasing public awareness of ASD in the community thanks to public education campaigns such as the Center for Disease Control and Prevention's Act Early campaign.

Within schools, early identification can occur as early as when children first become eligible for school-based services at age three years. ASD can be reliably diagnosed at this age. In fact, research indicates that ASD can be reliably diagnosed in children at the age of two years (Lord et al., 2006). Although autism can be reliably diagnosed at age two years and there seems to be a downward trend in the age of first diagnosis, many children are not diagnosed until after the age of three years and a fair number are identified only after they start school at the age of five years (Baio et al., 2018). In most cases, parents or professionals express concerns about a child's development before the age of three years, but it often takes a significant amount of time before a professional confirms a diagnosis of ASD (Christensen et al., 2016a, 2016b).

Schools play an important role in identifying children with ASD and find children who have not been identified by the health system. Educational records identify 38% more children with ASD than when medical records alone are considered (Pettygrove et al., 2013). Many children with ASD have been "missed" by the medical system, but they are identified by the schools. This is likely related to the fact that children have more equitable access to public schools than to healthcare. As might be expected, children identified by the schools tend to be older than those who are identified through the health system (Pettygrove et al., 2013).

Importance of early ASD intervention

Overall, the Center for Disease Control and Prevention's most recent reviews indicate that fewer than half of all children with ASD receive their first ASD evaluation before age three years (Baio et al., 2018). This indicates that most children do not receive an evaluation during the years when intervention is most effective. Research is beginning to show that, if children receive intervention while they are age three and under, later symptoms of ASD may be reduced (Dawson et al., 2010, 2012). These interventions focus on naturalistic applied behavioral strategies, deep parental involvement, and opportunities to address core social communication and emotional regulation deficits (Zwaigenbaum et al., 2015).

Identification of ASD across Diverse Populations

When people think of a child with an ASD, they often image a white male with an intellectual disability. Although this may be the picture of ASD in the past, we now know that ASD affects children of various racial, ethnic, and linguistic backgrounds as well as both males and females. ASD is reported to occur in all racial and ethnic groups (Christensen et al., 2016l). The identification of children across these demographics poses unique challenges and considerations.

Age of Identification Differences across Populations

Children with less severe symptoms of ASD and average cognitive abilities tend to be identified at later ages than children with intellectual disabilities (Christensen et al., 2016b; Mandell & Palmer, 2005). This is likely because children with intellectual disabilities miss developmental milestones in domains such as language and motor skills which are more closely monitored by pediatricians and noticed by parents. Parents tend to notice when their child's peers are talking and playing at the park, but theirs is not able to talk and climb on playground equipment. However, children with ASD without intellectual disabilities show more subtle differences in social communication which may be easier to miss. It may be only when an observant community preschool teacher or kindergarten teacher notices differences in a child's behavior that the assessment process is started.

Family-related factors can influence the age of diagnosis. Children from families with higher socioeconomic status tend to be identified earlier (Daniels & Mandell, 2014; Mandell & Palmer, 2005). This may be because these parents are more informed about developmental milestones or have better access to healthcare. However, children who are first born are often identified later than children with a later birth order within the family (Daniels & Mandell, 2014). This is likely because parents have a greater sense of typical development and become more concerned when a child born later in the birth order misses significant social–communication milestones.

> ### Case Study 1
>
> John is a 3 year old, white male. He is his parents' first child. He has been referred for a preschool evaluation for special needs preschool. His community preschool teacher recommended that John be evaluated after he had multiple "meltdowns" at school and his parents had to come to pick him up early. John's parents feel that the preschool is overreacting, but, as this is the second school that John has had difficulty at, they have agreed to an evaluation. John's parents note that he is very "smart;" he can already read short books. They wonder if he may be gifted and bored in his current preschool; perhaps this is causing his behavioral problems. He is the "apple of his parents' eyes" and they adapted their lives to make sure he is getting the best education and life experiences possible. He has passed all of the developmental screenings at his pediatrician's office.
>
> What factors may affect the length of time it takes for John to be identified as having ASD?
>
> What red flags are present to suggest a possible ASD should be considered by the school evaluation team?
>
> How would you approach parents who are feeling defensive that people are pointing out areas of possible weakness in their son?

Race also accounts for some differences in the age of diagnosis. Currently, white children are identified as having ASD at a higher rate than black and Hispanic children. The estimated prevalence of ASD for white children is 7% higher than black children and 22% higher than Hispanic children (Baio et al., 2018). In particular, Hispanic children tend to be evaluated for ASD at an older age than their peers (Christensen et al., 2016a). Similarly, within schools, Hispanic children are less likely to be eligible for special education in the area of ASD in schools (Locke et al., 2017). Although there are differences in the frequency with which children of different races/ethnicities are identified, there is no evidence to suggest that the actual rate of ASD is higher in white children. This means that the difference in current prevalence rates may be more related to identification processes and access to assessment services. Once children

- Lower socioeconomic status
- Hispanic
- First-born children
- Average cognitive abilities

Figure 3.1 Characteristics of children identified with ASD at a later age

qualify for services, the amount of money used to support them tends to be fairly equal, but it is their initial eligibility for services that varies (Locke et al., 2017).

In addition to differences in the age of diagnosis, socioeconomic and race/ethnicity factors are associated with differences in where children receive a diagnosis of ASD (Pettygrove et al., 2013). Some children are first assessed through the medical system whereas others are first assessed through the schools. Children from higher socioeconomic backgrounds are more likely to be assessed outside the school system, whereas those from lower socioeconomic backgrounds are more likely to be identified as first having ASD by the school system (Figure 3.1). School systems are also more likely to be the first to identify Hispanic children with ASD.

Families' experiences in the ASD diagnostic process vary. In general, families from diverse backgrounds have a less positive experience. Magaña, Parish, and Son (2015) found families from diverse backgrounds were less likely to feel that professionals listened to them, took the necessary time to explain their child's ASD to them, made them feel like a partner, and were sensitive to families' customs and values.

Bilingual Children with ASD

In 2014–15, approximately 9% or an estimated 4.6 million students in the public schools qualified as English language learners (McFarland et al., 2017). In the public schools, the most common foreign language is Spanish, with approximately 3.7 million speakers. Arabic, Chinese, and Vietnamese are the next most common home languages. Despite the large percentage of foreign language speakers in the USA, research examining bilingualism and ASD is relatively new. Given that children with ASD often present with delays in communication, it is imperative for educators to provide accurate recommendations to bilingual families.

Language Development in Bilingual Children with ASD

Although bilingualism and ASD is a newer area of research; studies thus far have consistently shown that introducing a second language to a child with ASD does not negatively affect the child's overall development. There is no greater language delay associated with bilingual exposure for children with ASD (Hambly & Fombonne, 2012; Peña, 2016). This is also true for bilingual children with language impairments, intellectual disabilities, and other developmental delays (Kay-Raining Bird, Genesee, & Verhoeven, 2016; Uljarević et al., 2016). Furthermore, pragmatic language (i.e., use of language for social purposes) is not negatively impacted by bilingual exposure (Reetzke et al., 2015). This is particularly relevant given that social communication is central to autism. Notably, the finding that bilingual exposure does not negatively affect any aspect of language has now been documented in toddlers, children, and adolescents with ASD. These studies have been conducted within a variety of cultural groups, including Spanish, French, and Chinese speakers (Drysdale, van der Meer, & Kagohara, 2015; Reetzke et al., 2015).

Preliminary findings suggest that bilingualism may provide some advantages for children with ASD. Bilingual children with ASD may use more gestures, engage in more cooing and pretend play, and have higher overall adaptive scores (Iarocci, Hutchison, & O'Toole, 2017; Valicenti-McDermott et al., 2013). There is also evidence that bilingualism may promote executive functioning, because children exposed to two languages must practice switching flexibly between languages and using perspective-taking to determine when to use which language (Iarocci et al., 2017; Peña, 2016). Overall, this means an ASD assessment should not be delayed for a bilingual child suspected of having an ASD. If a child's language is delayed in both English and their native language, this indicates a true delay rather than an issue of language acquisition.

Parental Experiences

Qualitative studies have found that bilingual parents of children with ASD are often worried that speaking more than one language at home may hinder their child's language development, cause confusion, and limit the child's access to services (Bird, Lamond, & Holden; Hampton et al., 2017; Yu, 2013). Although research has challenged these beliefs, studies find many parents have been advised by professionals to stop using their native language and communicate with their child only in English (Drysdale et al., 2015). However, there is no evidence to support the recommendation of switching to a monolingual English environment, and doing so may fail to consider important cultural factors.

Parents who are not native English speakers may find it uncomfortable and challenging to communicate with their child in English, which may in turn impact parent–child bonds (Hampton et al., 2017; Yu, 2013). Use of the child's native language is important because it allows for communication with non-English-speaking family members, participation in cultural and religious events, and connection with a cultural heritage

(Hampton et al., 2017). In summary, each language plays an important role in a child's life. Although the dominant language helps the child function in school and the community, the native language is important for familial bonds and cultural connection.

> **Tips for Talking with Parents**
>
> **Tips for Working with Bilingual Families of Children with ASD**
>
> Questions and facts to share with bilingual families:
>
> - Ask parents about their child's language use. (e.g., Who speaks in which languages at home? When did your child start to be exposed to English? What language does your child watch TV in?)
> - Research suggests that there is no reason not to use two languages to communicate with a child with autism.
> - Hearing or speaking two languages does not worsen language delays, reduce vocabulary size, confuse the child, or negatively impact his or her ability to communicate.
> - There is *preliminary* evidence that bilingualism may be beneficial. Bilingually exposed children with autism may engage in more gesturing and imaginative play and develop stronger executive functioning skills.
> - Talk with families about the personal nature of deciding whether to introduce a second language at home, reviewing possible pros and cons.
> - To support a child's home language: Provide ongoing exposure to the language, intentionally build vocabulary and grammar through everyday activities (reading books, talking about household activities), and link vocabulary to the demands of the home and school environment.
> - Therapy is beneficial when provided in English or the home language.

Supporting Language in Bilingual Children with ASD

For children with ASD, families also have to carefully consider whether it would benefit the child most to participate in therapy in English or the native language. The positive news is that research suggests that delivering intervention in either the native or the second language supports language growth (Peña, 2016). Native language intervention does not interfere with English acquisition as long as children still have opportunities to hear and practice English. Improving vocabulary and grammar in the native language may also positively affect the development of English

> **Case Study 2**
>
> Miguel is a 6-year-old boy. Spanish is his native language. He has not attended preschool. Miguel's teacher brings up concerns related to his speech. Miguel is able to name objects consistently in English, but he is not using more than two-word phrases. The ESOL teacher has also noted that his language progress is slow. His family reports that he is shy and does not speak much at home. Miguel's teacher has also noted that, although he runs around with the other children on the playground, he does not engage with them during center time in the classroom. He tends to play with blocks, building elaborate structures. Miguel has had a hard time with transitions between tasks in the classroom.
>
> What factors may be affecting the length of time it takes for Miguel to be identified as having ASD?
>
> Miguel's parents ask if they should try to speak only English at home. What is your response?
>
> A Spanish-speaking speech and language therapist is not available; how might this affect Miguel's language development?

Girls with ASD

Boys are about four times more likely to be diagnosed with ASD than girls (Baio et al., 2018). However, the difference in prevalence between boys and girls varies by children's intellectual abilities. There are fewer differences in prevalence by sex for children with ASD and an intellectual disability. But for children with more average cognitive ability and ASD, prevalence estimates suggest that 5–16 times more boys than girls are diagnosed with ASD (Dworzynski et al., 2012; Kreiser & White, 2014). This means that there are fewer girls identified with more average cognitive abilities.

There are also differences in the initial age at which girls are diagnosed with ASD versus boys. Recent studies show that girls may receive ASD diagnoses later than boys (Begeer et al., 2013; Giarelli et al., 2010). This is especially true for those girls with average cognitive abilities.

Why are Fewer Girls Diagnosed with ASD than boys?

There are a number of reasons that may explain why fewer girls are diagnosed with ASD than boys. Research is still being conducted to better understand these differences. There are likely biological reasons for the differences in prevalence by sex. Given the high heritability of ASD, one hypothesized reason for the higher prevalence of ASD in boys is due to genetic or biological reasons. The female protective effect indicates that being female provides a genetic advantage that protects girls from symptoms of autism (Robinson et al., 2013; Werling & Geschwind, 2015). Girls may have a higher threshold for genetic risk factors that have to be present in order to demonstrate ASD (Werling, 2016). Possible reasons for this protective effect might be related to girls having a second X chromosome or differences in hormone exposure.

Second, social–cultural expectations and biases have been theorized to contribute to differences in identification rates for girls and boys. The environment and therefore experiences of young girls and boys may vary, changing their developmental trajectory (Kreiser & White, 2014). Parents may shape children's behavior differently based on their child's gender. Parents may also encourage more social nurturing behavior in girls than in boys. For example, girls may be more likely to be given and taught how to play with dolls, learning to pretend to feed them and put them to bed. These early interactions and environmental differences may enhance the functioning of girls with ASD and make it more difficult to identify them; however, girls with ASD would be expected to still demonstrate significant social communication deficits. Parents' presenting concerns also show some differences across boys and girls. They report more concerns about boys' social interactions than girls' social interactions before a diagnosis of ASD (Little et al., 2017).

In addition, biases in assessment tools and criteria may make it more difficult to identify girls with ASD. Current diagnostic and symptom criteria may mask girls with ASD (Rynkiewicz et al., 2016), and they may be more aligned with boys' symptoms than girls' symptoms. When assessing a girl for an ASD, it is important to take into consideration gender differences between typically developing children. Young girls as a group demonstrate stronger social skills, e.g., in general, young girls are more interested in faces, show better imitation skills, demonstrate better eye contact, and engage in more cooperative play than boys (Andersson, Gillberg, & Miniscalco, 2013). Therefore, if girls with ASD are compared with boys with ASD rather than typically developing girls, some girls with ASD may be missed.

Girls with ASD may have a unique presentation that is different from boys' presentation. In studies of high-risk siblings' eye tracking, young girls who go on to be diagnosed with ASD show different patterns from young boys who go on to be diagnosed with ASD. Young girls show greater visual attention to social stimuli than young boys (Chawarska et al., 2016). In addition, research indicates that girls with ASD may demonstrate better nonverbal gestures and joint attention than boys (Øien et al., 2016; Rynkiewicz et al., 2016). Girls have demonstrated fewer restricted and repetitive behaviors than boys on measures such as

> - Compare girls to typically developing same-age *girls*, not to boys with ASD.
> - Girls with ASD may have fewer "acting out" behaviors than boys with ASD.
> - Look for restricted interests that are typical in content (e.g., Barbie, animals, fashion, Justin Bieber, "Frozen"), but unusual in intensity.
> - Girls may show fewer or less intense motor mannerisms (e.g., flapping, hand posturing, spinning).
> - Teenage girls with ASD may particularly lack insight into social roles, avoid social relationships, and have comorbid internalizing disorders (e.g., anxiety, depression).

Figure 3.2 Considerations when assessing girls for ASD

the ADOS and parent reports (Mandy et al., 2012; Tillmann et al., 2018). In addition, teachers report more externalizing and social problems for boys; therefore, girls with ASD symptoms may be less likely to stand out at school than boys (Hiller, Young, & Weber, 2014; Mandy et al., 2012). Furthermore, girls with ASD may have restricted interests that appear to be more normative in content (e.g., Justin Bieber, Minnie Mouse, My Little Pony, "Frozen") but are unusual in intensity. Some research also indicates that girls with ASD may show greater irritability than boys with ASD (Frazier et al., 2014).

Young girls' differences in symptomology may not prevent them from being diagnosed with ASD later, but it may change their trajectory and initial age of diagnosis. Even at the end of an evaluation, girls end up with an ASD diagnosis less frequently than boys, even with similarly high levels of ASD symptoms (Dworzynski et al., 2012; Russell, Steer, & Golding, 2011). This highlights the importance of increased research in this area to improve diagnostic tools.

Characteristics of Young Women with ASD

Young women with ASD in middle and high school might also present differently from young men with ASD. A qualitative study reported that young women with ASD are behaviorally rigid, socially ambivalent or avoidant, and lack insight with regard to peer relationships (Trubanova et al., 2014). In addition, young women with ASD may be more likely to experience comorbid internalizing disorders and sexual abuse (Bargiela, Steward, & Mandy, 2016). They also may be more likely to be diagnosed with an internalizing disorder rather than ASD.

Young women with ASD may also "camouflage" their ASD symptoms more than men, meaning that they may compensate or hide their autistic characteristics within social interactions (Hull et al., 2017; Ratto et al., 2018). For example, she may learn to look people in the eye because this is an expected behavior or she may try to prevent herself from showing repetitive behaviors. This camouflaging behavior can make identifying young women more difficult as well as contribute to the stress and anxiety they experience (Cage, Di Monaco, & Newell, 2018; Hull et al., 2017). Camouflaging behavior may also cause young women to be more likely to be missed in ASD assessments.

> **Case Study 3**
>
> Collette is a 9-year-old girl. She comes to your attention through a Response to Intervention (RTI) meeting due to behavioral problems. Her teacher expresses concerns about outbursts and poor work completion. Collette is described as being a "bossy" friend on the playground. When other children do not follow her rules, she complains to the teacher, and becomes upset, yelling, crying, and then withdrawing. This is occurring several times a week and it takes her approximately an hour to be able to move on. In the lunchroom, Collette becomes anxious and asks to leave. She does not eat her food and complains that the lunchroom is loud and smelly. Within the classroom, her teacher notices her frequently smelling her hands, the paper, and other objects. Academically, Collette is performing at grade level expectations, but she struggles to complete her work in class. Collette's parents report that she loves to play with My Little Pony and watches the same two television episodes repetitively. She also will wear only clothing that is predominantly pink.
>
> What factors may be affecting the length of time it takes for Collette to be identified as having ASD?
>
> Given that she is a girl, what considerations should you keep in mind if you evaluate her?

References

Andersson, G. W., Gillberg, C., & Miniscalco, C. (2013). Pre-school children with suspected autism spectrum disorders: Do girls and boys have the same profiles? *Research in Developmental Disabilities*, 34(1), 413–422. doi:http://dx.doi.org/10.1016/j.ridd.2012.08.025.

Baio, J., Wiggins, L., Christensen, D., Maenner, M. J., Daniels, J., Warren, Z., et al. (2018). Prevalence of autism spectrum disorder among children aged 8 years – Autism and Developmental Disabilities Monitoring Network, 11 sites, United States, 2014. *MMWR Surveillance Summary*, 67, 1–23. doi:http://dx.doi.org/10.15585/mmwr.ss6706a1.

Bargiela, S., Steward, R., & Mandy, W. (2016). The experiences of late-diagnosed women with autism spectrum conditions: An investigation of the female autism phenotype. *Journal of Autism & Developmental Disorders*, 46(10), 3281–3294. doi:10.1007/s10803-016-2872-8.

Begeer, S., Mandell, D., Wijnker-Holmes, B., Venderbosch, S., Rem, D., Stekelenburg, F., & Koot, H. M. (2013). Sex differences in the timing of identification among children and adults with autism spectrum disorders. *Journal of Autism and Developmental Disorders*, 43(5), 1151–1156. doi:10.1007/s10803-012-1656-z.

Bird, E. K. R., Lamond, E., & Holden, J. Survey of bilingualism in autism spectrum disorders. *International Journal of Language & Communication Disorder*, 47(1), 52–64. doi:10.1111/j.1460-6984.2011.00071.x.

Cage, E., Di Monaco, J., & Newell, V. (2018). Experiences of autism acceptance and mental health in autistic adults. *Journal of Autism and Developmental Disorders*, 48(2), 473–484. doi:10.1007/s10803-017-3342-7.

Chawarska, K., Macari, S., Powell, K., DiNicola, L., & Shic, F. (2016). Enhanced social attention in female infant siblings at risk for autism. *Journal of American Academy of Child and Adolescent Psychiatry*, 55(3), 188–195.e181. doi:10.1016/j.jaac.2015.11.016.

Christensen, D. L., Baio, J., Braun, K. V. N., Bilder, D., Charles, J., Constantino, J. N., et al. (2016a). Prevalence and characteristics of autism spectrum disorder among children aged 8 years – Autism and Developmental Disabilities Monitoring Network, 11 Sites, United States, 2012. *MMWR Surveillance Summaries*, 65(3), 1–23. doi:10.15585/mmwr.ss6503a1.

Christensen, D. L., Bilder, D. A., Zahorodny, W., Pettygrove, S., Durkin, M. S., Fitzgerald, R. T., et al. (2016b). Prevalence and characteristics of autism spectrum disorder among 4-year-old children in the Autism and Developmental Disabilities Monitoring Network. *Journal of Developmental Behavioral Pediatrics*, 37(1), 1–8. doi:10.1097/dbp.0000000000000235.

Daniels, A. M. & Mandell, D. S. (2014). Explaining differences in age at autism spectrum disorder diagnosis: a critical review. *Autism: International Journal of Research and Practice*, 18(5), 583–597. doi:10.1177/1362361313480277.

Dawson, G., Rogers, S., Munson, J., Smith, M., Winter, J., Greenson, J., et al. (2010). Randomized, controlled trial of an intervention for toddlers with autism: The Early Start Denver Model. *Pediatrics*, 125(1), 179.

Dawson, G., Jones, E.H., Merkle, K., Venema, K., Lowy, R., Faja, S., et al. (2012). Early behavioral intervention is associated with normalized brain activity in young children with autism. *American Academy of Child & Adolescent Psychiatry*, 51(11), 1150–1159. doi:10.1016/j.jaac.2012.08.018.

Drysdale, H., van der Meer, L., & Kagohara, D. (2015). Children with Autism Spectrum Disorder from bilingual families: A systematic review. *Review Journal of Autism & Developmental Disorders*, 2(1), 26–38. doi:10.1007/s40489-014-0032-7.

Dworzynski, K., Ronald, A., Bolton, P., & Happe, F. (2012). How different are girls and boys above and below the diagnostic threshold for autism spectrum disorders? *Journal of American Academy of Child & Adolescent Psychiatry*, 51(8), 788–797. doi:10.1016/j.jaac.2012.05.018.

Frazier, T. W., Georgiades, S., Bishop, S. L., & Hardan, A. Y. (2014). Behavioral and cognitive characteristics of females and males with autism in the Simons Simplex Collection. *Journal of the American Academy of Child & Adolescent Psychiatry*, 53(3), 329–340, e321–323. doi:10.1016/j.jaac.2013.12.004.

Giarelli, E., Wiggins, L.D., Rice, C.E., Levy, S.E., Kirby, R.S., Pinto-Martin, J., & Mandell, D. (2010). Sex differences in the evaluation and diagnosis of autism spectrum disorders among children. *Disability and Health Journal*, 3(2), 107–116. doi:10.1016/j.dhjo.2009.07.001.

Hambly, C. & Fombonne, E. (2012). The impact of bilingual environments on language development in children with autism spectrum disorders. *Journal of Autism and Developmental Disorders*, 42(7), 1342–1352. doi:10.1007/s10803-011-1365-z.

Hampton, S., Rabagliati, H., Sorace, A., & Fletcher-Watson, S. (2017). Autism and bilingualism: A qualitative interview study of parents' perspectives and experiences. *Journal of Speech, Language & Hearing Research*, 60, 435–446. doi:10.1044/2016_JSLHR-L-15-0348.

Hiller, R. M., Young, R. L., & Weber, N. (2014). Sex differences in autism spectrum disorder based on DSM-5 criteria: evidence from clinician and teacher reporting. *Journal of Abnormal Child Psychology*, 42(8), 1381–1393. doi:10.1007/s10802-014-9881-x.

Hull, L., Petrides, K. V., Allison, C., Smith, P., Baron-Cohen, S., Lai, M. C., & Mandy, W. (2017). "Putting on my best normal": Social camouflaging in adults with autism spectrum conditions. *Journal of Autism & Developmental Disorder*, 47(8), 2519–2534. doi:10.1007/s10803-017-3166-5.

Iarocci, G., Hutchison, S., & O'Toole, G. (2017). Second language exposure, functional communication, and executive function in children with and without autism spectrum disorder. *Journal of Autism & Developmental Disorders*, 47(6), 1818–1829. doi:10.1007/s10803-017-3103-7.

Kay-Raining Bird, E., Genesee, F., & Verhoeven, L. (2016). Bilingualism in children with developmental disorders: A narrative review. *Journal of Communication Disorders*, 63, 1–14. doi:http://dx.doi.org/10.1016/j.jcomdis.2016.07.003.

Kreiser, N. & White, S. (2014). ASD in females: Are we overstating the gender difference in diagnosis? *Clinical Child & Family Psychology Review*, 17(1), 67–84.

Little, L.M., Wallisch, A., Salley, B., & Jamison, R. (2017). Do early caregiver concerns differ for girls with autism spectrum disorders? *Autism: International Journal of Research & Practice*, 21(6), 728–732. doi:10.1177/1362361316664188.

Locke, J., Kang-Yi, C. D., Pellecchia, M., Marcus, S., Hadley, T., & Mandell, D. S. (2017). Ethnic disparities in school-based behavioral health service use for children with psychiatric disorders. *Journal of School Health*, 87(1), 47–54. doi:10.1111/josh.12469.

Lord, C., Risi, S., DiLavore, P.S., Shulman, C., Thurm, A., & Pickles, A. (2006). Autism from 2 to 9 years of age. *Archives of General Psychiatry*, 63(6), 694–701. doi:10.1001/archpsyc.63.6.694.

McFarland, J., Hussar, B., de Brey, C., Snyder, T., Wang, X., Wilkinson-Flicker, S., et al. (2017). *The Condition of Education 2017*. National Center for Education Statistics. Available at: https://nces.ed.gov/pubsearch/pubsinfo.asp?pubid=2017144 (accessed 1 August 2018).

Magaña, S., Parish, S. L., & Son, E. (2015). Have racial and ethnic disparities in the quality of health care relationships changed for children with developmental disabilities and ASD? *American Journal on Intellectual and Developmental Disabilities*, 120(6), 504–513. doi:10.1352/1944-7558-120.6.504.

Mandell, D. S. & Palmer, R. (2005). Differences among states in the identification of autistic spectrum disorders. *Archives of Pediatrics & Adolescent Medicine*, 159(3), 266–269. doi:10.1001/archpedi.159.3.266.

Mandy, W., Chilvers, R., Chowdhury, U., Salter, G., Seigal, A., & Skuse, D. (2012). Sex differences in autism spectrum disorder: Evidence from a large sample of children and adolescents. *Journal of Autism and Developmental Disorders*, 42(7), 1304–1313. doi:10.1007/s10803-011-1356-0.

Øien, R. A., Hart, L., Schjølberg, S., Wall, C. A., Kim, E. S., Nordahl-Hansen, A., et al. (2016). Parent-endorsed sex differences in toddlers with and without ASD: Utilizing the M-CHAT. *Journal of Autism and Developmental Disorders*, 1–9. doi:10.1007/s10803-016-2945-8

Peña, E.D. (2016). Supporting the home language of bilingual children with developmental disabilities: From knowing to doing. *Journal of Communication Disorders*, 63, 85–92. doi:10.1016/j.jcomdis.2016.08.001.

Pettygrove, S., Pinborough-Zimmerman, J., John Meaney, F., Naarden Braun, K., Nicholas, J., Miller, L., et al (2013). Predictors of ascertainment of Autism Spectrum Disorders across nine US communities. *Journal of Autism & Developmental Disorders*, 43(8), 1867–1879. doi:10.1007/s10803-012-1732-4.

Ratto, A. B., Kenworthy, L., Yerys, B. E., Bascom, J., Wieckowski, A. T., White, S. W., et al. (2018). What about the girls? Sex-based differences in autistic traits and adaptive skills. *Journal of Autism and Developmental Disorders*, 48(5), 1698–1711. doi:10.1007/s10803-017-3413-9.

Reetzke, R., Zou, X., Sheng, L., & Katsos, N. (2015). Communicative development in bilingually exposed Chinese children with autism spectrum disorders. *Journal of Speech, Language, and Hearing Research*, 58(3), 813–825.

Robinson, E. B., Lichtenstein, P., Anckarsäter, H., Happé, F., & Ronald, A. (2013). Examining and interpreting the female protective effect against autistic behavior. *Proceedings of the National Academy of Sciences of the USA*, 110(13), 5258–5262. doi:10.1073/pnas.1211070110.

Russell, G., Steer, C., & Golding, J. (2011). Social and demographic factors that influence the diagnosis of autistic spectrum disorders. *Social Psychiatry and Psychiatric Epidemiology*, 46(12), 1283–1293. doi:10.1007/s00127-010-0294-z.

Rynkiewicz, A., Schuller, B., Marchi, E., Piana, S., Camurri, A., Lassalle, A., & Baron-Cohen, S. (2016). An investigation of the "female camouflage effect" in autism using a computerized ADOS-2 and a test of sex/gender differences. *Molecular Autism*, 7, 10. doi:10.1186/s13229-016-0073-0.

Tillmann, J., Ashwood, K., Absoud, M., Bolte, S., Bonnet-Brilhault, F., Buitelaar, J. K., et al. (2018). Evaluating sex and age differences in ADI-R and ADOS scores in a large European multi-site sample of individuals with autism spectrum disorder. *Journal of Autism and Developmental Disorders*. doi:10.1007/s10803-018-3510-4

Trubanova, A., Donlon, K., Kreiser, N., Ollendick, T., & White, S. (2014). Underidentification of autism spectrum disorder in females: A case series illustrating the unique presentation of this disorder in young women. *Scandinavian Journal of Child and Adolescent Psychiatry and Psychology*, 2(2), 66–76.

Uljarević, M., Katsos, N., Hudry, K., & Gibson, J. L. (2016). Practitioner review: Multilingualism and neurodevelopmental disorders – an overview of recent research and discussion of clinical implications. *Journal of Child Psychology & Psychiatry*, 57(11), 1205–1217. doi:10.1111/jcpp.12596.

Valicenti-McDermott, M., Tarshis, N., Schouls, M., Galdston, M., Hottinger, K., Seijo, R., & Shinnar, S. (2013). Language differences between monolingual English and bilingual English–Spanish young children with autism spectrum disorders. *Journal Of Child Neurology*, 28(7), 945–948. doi:10.1177/0883073812453204.

Werling, D. M. (2016). The role of sex-differential biology in risk for autism spectrum disorder. *Biology and Sex Differences*, 7, 58. doi:10.1186/s13293-016-0112-8.

Werling, D. M. & Geschwind, D. H. (2015). Recurrence rates provide evidence for sex-differential, familial genetic liability for autism spectrum disorders in multiplex families and twins. *Molecular Autism*, 6, 27. doi:10.1186/s13229-015-0004-5.

Yu, B. (2013). Issues in bilingualism and heritage language maintenance: perspectives of minority-language mothers of children with autism spectrum disorders. *American Journal of Speech–Language Pathology/American Speech–Language–Hearing Association*, 22(1), 10–24. doi:10.1044/1058-0360(2012/10-0078).

Zwaigenbaum, L., Bauman, M. L., Choueiri, R., Kasari, C., Carter, A., Granpeesheh, D., et al. (2015). Early intervention for children with autism spectrum disorder under 3 years of age: Recommendations for practice and research. *Pediatrics*, 136, S60–S81. doi:10.1542/peds.2014-3667E.

Chapter 4
Comorbid Conditions and Disorders

While autism spectrum disorders (ASD) are defined by deficits in social–communication skills and repetitive/restricted interests and behaviors, children with ASD also demonstrate a number of other problems that affect their school functioning, behavior, health, and well-being. These problems include medical conditions, psychiatric disorders, cognitive differences, and related concerns. Knowing that a child has difficulties, or a history of problems, in these areas can provide school psychologists with data to inform their evaluations and eligibility recommendations. This underscores the importance of obtaining a thorough developmental history. School psychologists may be able to provide important information to parents which helps identify comorbid conditions and important intervention strategies that will allow their child to achieve better long-term outcomes. In addition to comorbid conditions, several conditions or disorders below may be the primary cause of a child's difficulties. This highlights the importance of differentiating between ASD and other disorders that may share some symptoms.

Medical Conditions

Seizure Disorders

Children with ASD have a significantly higher risk of epilepsy than the general population risk of 1–2%. The precise prevalence rates of epilepsy in children with ASD is unknown; however, estimates range from 5% to 46% (Bryson, Clark & Smith 1988; Hughes, 2005; Kanner, 1943; Thomas et al., 2017). One reason that the range is so broad is that the causes of autism are heterogeneous. In some cases, ASD has a known cause that may include a gene defect or syndrome that is related to a high risk for seizures. For the general group of children with ASD, the risk of seizures is described as 30%. However, for children with ASD who do not have a known syndrome that carries a higher risk for epilepsy, the risk of a seizure disorder is about 10–15% (Spence & Schneider, 2009).

In addition, girls with ASD in particular may have a higher risk of seizures (Thomas et al., 2017)

The diagnosis of seizure activity in children with ASD can be difficult because many of the behavioral symptoms of complex partial and/or absence seizures, such as staring, non-responsiveness, and repetitive motor behaviors, mirror the behaviors often seen in ASD. Nevertheless, it is important for parents and teachers of individuals with ASD to be mindful of the higher risk for epilepsy, and to raise concerns if a child experiences periods in which he or she is nonresponsive, particularly if the child does not respond when touched. When any concerning behavior is observed, a consultation with the child's pediatrician and possibly a neurologist is recommended.

Visual and Hearing Impairments

Hearing and vision tests should routinely be completed before ASD assessments to rule out visual impairments (VIs) and hearing impairments (HIs) that may cause a child's developmental differences. However, it should be noted that ASD can co-occur in children with VIs and HIs. Do et al. (2017) estimated the prevalence of ASD in VI and HI populations as 19% and 9%, respectively. Although the rates of co-occurrence of ASD with VI or HI may be elevated, practitioners can be hesitant to also identify ASD, believing that the sensory impairment is the primary concern that is affecting the child's social communication and behaviors (Jure, Pogonza & Rapin, 2016).

In VI populations, children with retinopathy of prematurity or congenital blindness may demonstrate a particularly high likelihood of co-occurring ASD (Jure et al., 2016). In HI populations, it is particularly important to consider a child's social functioning and the presence of repetitive/restricted behaviors as a child with an HI may be expected to have language delays. Studies have shown that ASD-specific assessments can differentiate between children with HI and those with ASD (Worley, Matson & Kozlowski, 2011).

Case Study 1

Steven is an 8-year-old boy in the third grade. He was eligible for special education in the areas of moderate intellectual disability, speech–language impairment, and visual impairment. He was referred for a re-evaluation because he was making academic progress and the team questioned if his moderate intellectual disability eligibility was correct.

(continued)

> *(continued)*
>
> Steven has diagnoses of nystagmus and optic nerve hypoplasia. A vision exam indicated he could see and reach for a flashlight, but he did not show interest in following the flashlight horizontally or vertically. He did not have a response to visual threat. Steven tended to lead with his left eye to explore his environment.
>
> Steven engages in stereotyped behaviors. He will spin in circles with his arms up as well as flap his arms. He will also "smack high five to the air." Steven bangs his head against toys or the door. He will also hit his hand into his teeth. Steven's mother described him as "Mozart on the piano." He is able to name the artist of a song after hearing three notes. He has an excellent memory.
>
> Steven has problems with sleeping. He can stay awake for two or three days at a time. Currently, he goes to bed between 9:30 and 10pm and gets up at 6am on school days. He takes Benadryl to help him sleep. Since Steven has started school, he is exhausted when he gets home. Steven eats with his fingers. He loves fruit. Steven does not like sauces or mash potatoes. He will eat some meat, but he does not like beef.
>
> During assessment, Steven used repetitive phrases such as "Want a starfish?" Some of his verbalizations did not have a clear intent. He was able to follow some simple directions such as, "Sit down." Throughout assessment sessions, Steven repetitively directed the examiner to spell words. When the examiner directed him to spell the words, he could spell words such as expert, cake, and twist. At one point, Steven tried to use the examiner's hand to scratch an itch that he had on his leg. He exhibited some laughter at inappropriate times or at times when there was no clear antecedent.
>
> How would you adapt your assessment for Steven's visual impairment?
>
> What symptoms would you be looking for in order to consider a co-occurring ASD eligibility?

Additional Health Concerns

Children with ASD demonstrate a greater risk for a number of health-related problems. In particular, rates of headaches/migraines, respiratory, food allergies, ear infections, and gastrointestinal symptoms, such as diarrhea or constipation, are higher in children with ASD (Adams et al., 2016; Schieve et al., 2012). Children with ASD and other neurodevelopmental disorders also tend to show higher rates of congenital heart disorders (Jin et al., 2017).

Intellectual Functioning

Intellectual Disability

An intellectual disability (ID) is defined as significantly delayed intellectual functioning demonstrated by an intelligence quotient (IQ) of 70 or below, as well as deficits or impairments in adaptive functioning. Historically, autism spectrum disorder was considered to be highly associated with intellectual disability; however, recent studies are showing much less overlap between the two conditions. The Autism Developmental Disabilities Monitoring Network found that, in 2014, 31% of children with ASD were classified in the range of intellectual disability (i.e., IQ <70), 25% were in the borderline range (i.e., IQ 71–85), and 44% had IQ scores in the average to above average range (i.e., IQ >85; Baio et al., 2018). This is a significant shift from earlier studies, even as recently as 2002, in which approximately 50% of children with ASD had IQs in the ID range (Durkin et al., 2017). This trend toward lower rates of ID has been even more pronounced for girls. The rates of ID for girls went from 60% in 2000–2 to 36% in 2014 (Baio et al., 2018; Durkin et al., 2017). These lower rates likely reflect better detection of high functioning autism, as well as the positive outcomes associated with early detection and intervention.

It should be noted that, in many cases, especially with very young children, it is important to differentiate between a child who has an ID rather than an ASD. When evaluating a young toddler or preschooler, clinical judgment is needed to carefully determine whether the social and communication deficits are above and beyond what would be expected based on the child's developmental level. Social delays that are consistent with an overall global developmental delay may not indicate a specific social vulnerability characteristic of ASD.

Giftedness

Some children with ASD may have an exceptionally high IQ, qualifying them for services in the area of "gifted." They are considered twice exceptional. The prevalence of the co-occurrence of ASD and giftedness is unknown. Finding the appropriate educational placements for children who are gifted and have ASD can be challenging (Rubenstein et al., 2015). Although they need challenging academic environments that allow for creativity, they simultaneously need additional support socially and adaptively. Gifted children with ASD tend to have more internalizing and externalizing behaviors than their gifted peers without ASD, as well as more difficulties with adaptive behaviors and executive functioning (Assouline, Nicpon, & Doobay, 2009; Foley-Nicpon, Doobay, & Assouline, 2010).

However, some of these difficulties may decrease over time (Foley-Nicpon et al., 2010). Further, it may be particularly easy to miss the presence of ASD in girls who are also gifted (Assouline et al., 2009).

Psychiatric Disorders

Children with ASD have been reported to have psychiatric disorders at rates that are four to six times higher than those reported in the general population (Costello et al., 2003). Therefore, children may have not only ASD, but also anxiety, depression, attention-deficit hyperactivity disorder (ADHD), aggressive behaviors, and/or schizophrenia. Children with comorbid conditions show symptoms of these disorders over and above what would be expected for a child with ASD. For example, ADHD would not be considered in addition to ASD unless the child's hyperactivity and inattention were significantly more of a problem than in most children with ASD. These comorbid conditions are evident in elementary age children as well as adolescents. Children with ASD and comorbid psychiatric disorders may be eligible for special education in the area of ASD as well as emotional behavioral disorder or other health impairment.

Anxiety

Anxiety is the most common psychiatric disorder to co-occur in children with ASD. Studies indicate that between 43% and 84% of children with ASD also meet criteria for an anxiety disorder (De Bruin et al., 2007; Leyfer et al., 2006; Muris et al., 1998; Salazar et al., 2015). Anxiety may be generalized, or related to specific phobias, social anxiety, or separation anxiety (White et al., 2009). Although all children with ASD may be at greater risk for developing problems with anxiety, children with ASD and average levels of cognitive abilities may be at particular risk (White et al., 2009), possibly because they are able to recognize their differences from their peers more.

There are many contributing factors to these high rates of anxiety. Children with ASD tend to be particularly stressed by transitions and change due to their inflexibility. Thus, they often become fearful of anticipated changes. Fear of aversive sensory stimuli can also lead to high levels of anxiety. In addition, given the social vulnerability that is inherent to ASD, the social demands of typical childhood and school activities can lead to sustained fear, apprehension, and worry of responding incorrectly. Furthermore, efforts to camouflage ASD symptoms may contribute to the stress children feel. To compound the issue, many individuals with ASD do not have adequate coping skills to handle these chronic stressors. Therefore, it is very important to monitor these children for anxiety and to help support their learning of emotional coping skills. When anxiety symptoms are present, ongoing counseling can be very helpful. Cognitive–behavioral therapy is an effective form of intervention (McNally Keehn et al, 2013; Sukhodolsky et al, 2013). Medication is often also used to help control anxiety symptoms.

Depression

In addition to anxiety, many children with ASD experience high rates of depression. Previous studies indicate that the rates of depression for children and adolescents with ASD range from 11% to 30% (De Bruin et al., 2007; Leyfer et al., 2006; Wing, 1981). There are many contributing factors to depression symptoms. Difficulties with social interaction can result in social isolation. Furthermore, children with ASD can be self-critical and unable to tolerate making mistakes. Temper outbursts can be a common reaction to stress and frustration, which leads to difficulties in school and home environments that can compound feelings of hopelessness. In addition, factors such as higher cognitive abilities, greater self-awareness of differences, increased ability for introspection, adolescence, weaker relationships, and difficulties describing emotions can contribute to greater depressive symptoms (De-la-Iglesia & Olivar, 2015). Suicidality is increased in children and adolescents with ASD. Suicidal ideation has been measured as present in 10–50% of youth with ASD (Segers & Rawana, 2014). This highlights the importance of assessing for suicidality in all children and youth with ASD.

Similar to children with anxiety, cognitive–behavioral therapy can help to alleviate depression symptoms that are comorbid with ASD (McGillivray & Evert, 2014). Medication is also sometimes used, although there are not many well-controlled studies of its effectiveness (Mohiuddin & Ghaziuddin, 2013).

Attention-deficit Hyperactivity Disorder

Many children with ASD also present with symptoms of attention-deficit hyperactivity disorder (ADHD), with some studies showing rates as high as 59% (Salazar et al., 2015). The relationship between ADHD and ASD can be complicated because many children with ASD often present with hyperactivity and impulsivity, as well as attentional differences

Table 4.1 Factors associated with increased risk for comorbid anxiety and depression

- Adolescence
- Higher cognitive abilities
- Increased awareness of differences
- Difficulty understanding emotions
- Poor social relationships

or executive functioning difficulties. Research has shown that ADHD symptoms can mask symptoms of ASD. ADHD is often identified before an ASD is identified (Soke et al., 2018). Frenette et al. (2013) found that children with ASD and co-occurring ADHD symptoms were identified 1.29 years later than those who did not have ADHD symptoms. Hyperactive and impulsive behaviors are likely to be disruptive in many environments and thus may be more readily identified than the social vulnerabilities that are the key feature of ASD.

Many of the intervention strategies that are useful for children with ASD are also helpful to address inattention, hyperactivity, and impulsivity. This includes the use of visual schedules, increased structure, clear boundaries and expectations, and frequent positive reinforcement for on-task behaviors. In order to control symptoms of comorbid ADHD, stimulant medication can be used (Pearson et al., 2013; Sturman, Deckx, & van Driel, 2017). Children with ASD and ADHD may not benefit as much from social skills groups as children with ASD alone (Taurines et al., 2012).

Case Study 2

Derrick is a sixth-grade boy. He has been eligible for special education in the area of Other Health Impaired due to ADHD since second grade. His special education teacher comes to you to talk about his reevaluation. Derrick has been having a lot of problems. He often fails to finish his independent work and needs constant prompts from his teacher. Derrick does not have any friends in his classes. He complains that "No one likes me," and says, "I'm a loser." He likes to hang around his teacher. When his teacher tries to engage with him, his eye contact is low and voice monotone. He cannot keep a conversation going unless it is about rocks and minerals. He tends to keep to himself and read books about rocks and minerals. In addition, he often sulks and appears to have low energy. He has become increasingly irritable. Derrick tends to have a lot of difficulty when his teacher is out, there is an assembly, or the class goes on a field trip. He will become agitated and get in trouble for disrupting the class by yelling and crying. He is constantly complaining that the classroom lights are too bright, and that he cannot concentrate.

What additional information would you want to consider an ASD eligibility?

What comorbid conditions might you consider?

What factors might put Derrick at risk for comorbid depressive symptoms?

Obsessive–Compulsive Disorder

Differential diagnoses between obsessive–compulsive disorder (OCD) and ASD can be tricky. Research does not indicate that OCD and ASD frequently co-occur, although their symptoms can be similar. Often, when talking about their child's symptoms, parents of children with ASD talk about their child's many "OCD behaviors." These include rigid adherence to routines, restricted interests, and ritualized or repetitive verbalizations. However, to determine whether a child truly has an OCD, it is important to distinguish between obsessive thoughts versus circumscribed interests, as well as compulsive behaviors versus restricted or repetitive behaviors (Saulnier & Ventola, 2012; Sparrow, Ciccheti, & Saulnier, 2016).

Obsessions in OCD are recurrent and persistent thoughts, urges, or images that are experienced as intrusive and inappropriate, and cause marked anxiety and distress. However, in ASD, circumscribed interests or "obsessions" are not experienced as distressing, and instead might actually alleviate anxiety and help a child to self-regulate. Compulsions are repetitive behaviors (e.g., hand washing, ordering, checking) or mental acts (e.g., praying, counting, repeating words silently) that a child feels he or she must perform in response to an obsession or according to rules that must be applied rigidly. A key component of a compulsion in OCD is that the behavior or action is aimed at preventing or reducing anxiety/distress. The repetitive behaviors seen in ASD are not typically tied to a particular obsession or worry, but they are more likely related to the child's natural interests. Thus, OCD is often an important differential diagnosis for children presenting with repetitive behaviors and persistent thoughts; however, it is not frequently comorbid.

Aggressive Behavior

The combination of rigid thinking, low frustration tolerance, high anxiety, sensory sensitivities, and poor communication skills can lead to maladaptive behaviors such as aggression and self-injury. Estimates suggest that 30–50% of children with ASD demonstrate some symptoms of aggression (Hartley, Sikora, & McCoy, 2008; Kanne & Mazurek, 2011; Mazurek, Kanne, & Wodka, 2013). Aggression can be associated with other clinical features including sleep problems, sensory problems, gastrointestinal (GI) problems, and communication and social functioning problems (Mazurek et al., 2013). In addition, younger children are more likely than older children and adolescents to engage in aggressive behaviors.

Individuals with ASD who are younger come from higher-income families, have more parent reported social/communication problems, or engage in repetitive behaviors more likely to demonstrate aggression (Kanne & Mazurek, 2011). Children with ASD, weaker adaptive skills, and lower cognitive abilities tend to show more aggressive behaviors (Farmer et al., 2015). For many children, aggressive behaviors decrease as their ability to communicate their wants and needs increases. These findings highlight the need to consider a child's other clinical symptoms when developing treatment strategies to manage aggression.

Finally, if a child demonstrates possible ASD symptoms as well as aggressive behaviors and has been exposed to abuse or neglect, careful differential considerations are important. Although a child can be in foster care and have ASD, the effects of abuse and neglect can cause differences in child's behavior and social attachments that are not due to an ASD. On the other hand, the child may truly have ASD and the disability may have been a risk factor for placement outside the parents' care (Cidav, Xie, & Mandell, 2018).

Schizophrenia

There is a subset of individuals with autism who begin to demonstrate psychotic symptoms in adolescence, although it is difficult to know the true prevalence of schizophrenia in children with ASD (Khandaker et al., 2014).

A differential diagnosis between ASD and schizophrenia can be difficult. One reason is that, at face value, many of the symptoms of a prodromal state of schizophrenia are similar to the symptoms of ASD. The prodromal stage of schizophrenia is the early stage that precedes psychotic symptoms such as hallucinations and delusions. Common prodromal symptoms include social withdrawal, poor eye contact, limited facial expressions of emotions, a marked drop in functioning, uncharacteristic behavior, increasing difficulty with concentration, loss of motivation to participate in any activity, dramatic sleep and appetite changes, suspiciousness of others, unusual or exaggerated beliefs about personal powers or influences, unusual thinking, and limited facial expressions of emotions (Fusar-Poli et al., 2013). In addition, symptoms of ASD can be misinterpreted as symptoms of a thought disorder, rigidity and difficulty with change can present as paranoia, and delayed echolalia, and poor pragmatic language skills can present as loose associations that are associated with a thought disorder (Hofvander et al., 2009; Konstantareas & Hewitt, 2001).

A child's early developmental history is important when differentiating ASD from an emerging thought disorder or determining if the two disorders are co-occurring. ASD symptoms are present in early childhood;

however, schizophrenia symptoms tend to emerge in later adolescence. When schizophrenia is comorbid with ASD, the child's developmental history will include marked difficulties with social communication and interaction, as well as repetitive behaviors early in development, with co-occurring emergence of hallucinations and delusions at a later stage in development.

Related Problems

Sleep

Children with ASD often experience problems with sleep. It is estimated that 44–83% of children with ASD have sleep problems (Goldman et al., 2009). In particular, they often have sleep-onset insomnia and nocturnal awakenings. Difficulties with sleep for children with ASD can be associated with increases in social skills deficits, ADHD, and repetitive behaviors (Malow et al., 2012). Furthermore, children's problems with falling asleep and staying asleep can disrupt the entire family's sleep patterns and cause significant distress (Malow et al., 2012). In many cases, helping to establish healthier sleep patterns can be an important first step in improving overall behavioral regulation. The following guidelines for healthy sleep hygiene are recommended by the US National Institutes of Health:

- Set a regular time for bed each night and stick to it. This should allow the child to receive 10–12 hours of sleep each night.
- Allow children to sleep in their own bed and learn to self-sooth during sleep.
- Establish a relaxing bedtime routine, such as giving your child a warm bath or reading him or her a story.
- Make after-dinner playtime a relaxing time. Too much activity close to bedtime can keep a child awake.
- Provide a quiet, darkened space for your child to sleep. Do not allow your child to have a TV or radio on at bedtime, because the changes in light and sound will keep your child from a deep restful sleep.

Although these guidelines can be a helpful first start, the sleep challenges present in children with ASD are often above and beyond typical childhood sleep problems. Treatments also involve the use of behavioral interventions and melatonin, both of which have empirical support for improving the sleep habits of children with ASD (Malow et al., 2012, 2016; Tilford et al., 2015).

> **Tips for Talking with Families 1**
>
> **Resources to Aid with Sleep Problems**
>
> Autism Speaks Sleep Toolkits:
>
> - Parent's Guide to Improving Sleep in Children with Autism and Sleep Strategies for Teens with Autism Spectrum Disorder: A Guide for Parents!: https://www.autismspeaks.org/science/resources-programs/autism-treatment-network/tools-you-can-use/sleep-tool-kit
> - ATN/AIR-P Melatonin and Sleep Problems: A Guide for Parents: https://www.autismspeaks.org/science/find-resources-programs/autism-treatment-network/tools-you-can-use/atn-air-p-melatonin-sleep-problems
>
> Book Recommendation:
>
> - *Sleep Better!: A Guide to Improving Sleep for Children with Special Needs*, Revised edition by Mark Durand.

Feeding

Up to 40% of all children experience some mealtime difficulties; however, within children with ASD, 46–89% of children experience significant feeding atypicalities (Sharp et al., 2010, 2013). Children with ASD may refuse foods, causing reduced volume of food to be eaten, or they may demonstrate food selectivity, causing a reduced variety of foods to be eaten. Some children show a combination of these two problems. Children with ASD often prefer foods high in carbohydrates, snacks, fats, and/or processed food. Fruits and vegetables are often rejected. In addition, they tend to consume lower amounts of calcium and protein. Some children with ASD develop rituals or very rigid thinking related to food. For example, they may eat only one brand of macaroni and cheese or only foods that are one particular color. Often the preferred foods are related to specific texture preferences or aversions. These feeding difficulties are associated with many health problems, including vitamin deficiencies, failure to thrive, and constipation. Children with ASD who present with feeding difficulties should be referred to a feeding specialist or GI doctor to rule out any possible underlying GI issues. Once medical explanations have been ruled out, behavioral interventions have the most empirical support for improving feeding problems (Sharp et al., 2010).

Problem behaviors at mealtimes also tend to affect the entire family, serving to disrupt what might otherwise be an ideal opportunity for social interaction and conversation together as a family. The disruption of this natural context for social interaction can result in further social isolation for the individual with ASD and fewer opportunities to practice communication strategies. At school, feeding difficulties can lead to problem behaviors during lunchtime and increased peer problems. Furthermore, children with ASD may avoid eating at school, which serves to further exacerbate behavioral dysregulation towards the end of the day.

Elopement

In recent years, safety issues affecting children with ASD have drawn increased attention. In particular, 26–49% of children with ASD wander off or elope (Kiely et al., 2016; Rice et al., 2016). Children with ASD are known to wander at home, in stores, and at school. Some children are drawn to water, which is especially dangerous due to the possibility of drowning. Children with ASD and intellectual disabilities are at increased risk of wandering away. Due to their weaknesses in communication, social deficits, unusual interests, and possible weak reasoning skills, children with ASD can be at higher risk for becoming lost or injured when they wander. Screening for safety concerns is important within an assessment.

Wandering behavior is very stressful for parents and teachers. Studies indicate that 58% of parents rank wandering among the most stressful ASD behaviors, and 62% of families of children who elope were prevented from attending/enjoying activities outside the home (*Interactive Autism Network Report: Elopement and Wandering*, Law & Anderson, 2011).

Tips for Talking with Families 2

Resources to Increase Safety

Resources for helping to keep children safe include the following:
- National Autism Association Safety Tools: http://nationalautismassociation.org
    - NAA's Be REDy Booklet for Teachers
    - Big Red Safety Box for Families – free kit with practical tools
- Safety products: https://www.autismspeaks.org/family-services/resource-library/safety-products

References

Adams, D., Susi, A., Erdie-Lalena, C., Gorman, G., Hisle-Gorman, E., Rajnik, M., et al. (2016). Otitis media and related complications among children with autism spectrum disorders. *Journal of Autism & Developmental Disorders*, 46(5), 1636–1642. doi:10.1007/s10803-015-2689-x.

Assouline, S. G., Nicpon, M. F., & Doobay, A. (2009). Profoundly gifted girls and autism spectrum disorder. *Gifted Child Quarterly*, 53(2), 89–105.

Baio, J., Wiggins, L., Christensen, D. L., Maenner, M., Daniels, J., Warren, Z., et al. (2018). Prevalence of autism spectrum disorder among children aged 8 years — Autism and Developmental Disabilities Monitoring Network, 11 sites, United States, 2014. *Mortality and Morbidity Weekly Report Surveillance Summaries*, 67, 1–23. doi:http://dx.doi.org/10.15585/mmwr.ss6706a1.

Bryson SE, Clark, B. & Smith IM. (1988). First report of a Canadian epidemiological study of autistic syndromes. *Journal of Child Psychology and Psychiatry*, 29, 433–445.

Cidav, Z., Xie, M., & Mandell, D. (2018). Foster care involvement among Medicaid-enrolled children with Autism. *Journal of Autism & Developmental Disorders*, 48(1), 176–183. doi:10.1007/s10803-017-3311-1.

Costello, E. J., Mustillo, S., Erkanli, A., Keeler, G., & Angold, A. (2003). Prevalence and development of psychiatric disorders in childhood and adolescence. *Archives of General Psychiatry*, 60(8), 837–844.

De-la-Iglesia, M. & Olivar, J. S. (2015). Risk factors for depression in children and adolescents with high functioning autism spectrum disorders. *Scientific World Journal*, doi:10.1155/2015/127853.

De Bruin, E. I., Ferdinand, R. F., Meester, S., de Nijs, P. F. A., & Verheij, F. (2007). High rates of psychiatric co-morbidity in PDD-NOS. *Journal of Autism & Developmental Disorders*, 37, 877–886.

Do, B., Lynch, P., Macris, E.M., Smyth, B., Stavrinakis, S., Quinn, S., & Constable, P.A. (2017). Systematic review and meta-analysis of the association of autism spectrum disorder in visually or hearing impaired children. *Ophthalmic Physiological Optics*, 37(2), 212–224.

Durkin, M. S., Maenner, M. J., Baio, J., Christensen, D., Daniels, J., Fitzgerald, R., et al. (2017). Autism spectrum disorder among US children (2002–2010): socioeconomic, racial, and ethnic disparities. *American Journal of Public Health*, 107(11), 1818–1826. doi:10.2105/ajph.2017.304032.

Farmer, C., Butter, E., Mazurek, M. O., Cowan, C., Lainhart, J., Cook, E. H., et al. (2015). Aggression in children with autism spectrum disorders and a clinic-referred comparison group. *Autism*, 19(3), 281–291. doi:10.1177/1362361313518995.

Foley-Nicpon, M., Doobay, A.F., & Assouline, S. G. (2010). Parent, teacher, and self perceptions of psychosocial functioning in intellectually gifted children and adolescents with autism spectrum disorder. *Journal of Autism Developmental Disorders*, 40(8), 1028–1038. doi:10.1007/s10803-010-0952-8.

Frenette, P., Dodds, L., MacPherson, K., Flowerdew, G., & Bryson, S. (2013). Factors affecting the age at diagnosis of autism spectrum disorders in Nova Scotia, Canada. *Autism*, 17(2), 184–195.

Fusar-Poli, P., Borgwardt, S., Bechdolf, A., Addington, J., Riecher-Rossler, A., Schultze-Lutter, F., et al. (2013). The psychosis high-risk state: a comprehensive state-of-the-art review. *JAMA Psychiatry*, 70(1), 107–120. doi:10.1001/jamapsychiatry.2013.269.

Goldman, S. E., Surdyka, K., Cuevas, R., Adkins, K., Wang, L., & Malow, B. A. (2009). Defining the sleep phenotype in children with autism. *Developmental Neuropsychology*, 34(5), 560–573. doi:10.1080/87565640903133509.

Hartley, S. L., Sikora, D. M., & McCoy, R. (2008). Prevalence and risk factors of maladaptive behaviour in young children with autistic disorder. *Journal of Intellectual Disability Research*, 52(10), 819–829. doi:10.1111/j.1365-2788.2008.01065.x.

Hofvander, B., Delorme, R., Chaste, P., Nyden, A., Wentz, E., Stahlberg, O., et al. (2009). Psychiatric and psychosocial problems in adults with normal-intelligence autism spectrum disorders. *BMC Psychiatry*, 9, 35. doi:10.1186/1471-244x-9-35.

Hughes Jr, M. M. (2005). EEG and seizures in autistic children and adolescents: further findings with therapeutic implications. *Clinical EEG Neuroscience*, 36, 15–20.

Jin, S. C., Homsy, J., Zaidi, S., Lu, Q., Morton, S., DePalma, S. R., et al.. (2017). Contribution of rare inherited and de novo variants in 2,871 congenital heart disease probands. *Nature Genetics*, 49(11), 1593–1601. doi:10.1038/ng.3970.

Jure, R., Pogonza, R., & Rapin, I. (2016). Autism spectrum disorders (ASD) in blind children: Very high prevalence, potentially better outlook. *Journal of Autism & Developmental Disorders*, 46(3), 749–759. doi:10.1007/s10803-015-2612-5.

Kanne, S. M. & Mazurek, M. O. (2011). Aggression in children and adolescents with ASD: prevalence and risk factors. *Journal of Autism & Developmental Disorders*, 41(7), 926–937. doi:10.1007/s10803-010-1118-4.

Kanner, L. (1943). Autistic disturbances of affective contact. *Nervous Child*, 2, 217–250.

Khandaker, G. M., Stochl, J., Zammit, S., Lewis, G., & Jones, P. B. (2014). A population-based longitudinal study of childhood neurodevelopmental disorders, IQ and subsequent risk of psychotic experiences in adolescence. *Psychological Medicine*, 44, 3229–3238.

Kiely, B., Migdal, T. R., Vettam, S., & Adesman, A. (2016). Prevalence and correlates of elopement in a nationally representative sample of children with developmental disabilities in the United States. *PloS one*, 11(2), 1–11.

Konstantareas, M. M. & Hewitt, T. (2001). Autistic disorder and schizophrenia: diagnostic overlaps. *Journal of Autism & Developmental Disorders*, 31(1), 19–28.

Law, P. & Anderson, C. (2011). *Elopement and Wandering*, Report. Baltimore, MA: Interactive Autism Network.

Leyfer, O. T., Folstein, S. E., Bacalman, S., Davis, N. O., Dinh, E., Morgan, J., et al. (2006). Comorbid psychiatric disorders in children with autism: interview development and rates of disorders. *Journal of Autism & Developmental Disorders*, 36, 849–861.

McGillivray, J. A. & Evert, H. T. (2014). Group cognitive behavioural therapy program shows potential in reducing symptoms of depression and stress among young people with ASD. *Journal of Autism & Developmental Disorders*, 44(8), 2041–2051. doi:10.1007/s10803-014-2087-9.

McNally Keehn, R. H., Lincoln, A. J., Brown, M. Z., & Chavira, D. A. (2013). The Coping Cat program for children with anxiety and autism spectrum disorder: a pilot randomized controlled trial. *Journal of Autism & Developmental Disorders*, 43(1), 57–67. doi:10.1007/s10803-012-1541-9.

Malow, B., Adkins, K., McGrew, S., Wang, L., Goldman, S., Fawkes, D., & Burnette, C. (2012). Melatonin for sleep in children with autism: A controlled trial examining dose, tolerability, and outcomes. *Journal of Autism & Developmental Disorders*, 42(8), 1729–1737. doi:10.1007/s10803-011-1418-3.

Malow, B. A., Katz, T., Reynolds, A. M., Shui, A., Carno, M., Connolly, H. V., et al. (2016). Sleep difficulties and medications in children with autism spectrum disorders: A registry study. *Pediatrics*, 137(Suppl 2), S98–S104. doi:10.1542/peds.2015-2851H.

Mazurek, M. O., Kanne, S. M., & Wodka, E. L. (2013). Physical aggression in children and adolescents with autism spectrum disorders. *Research in Autism Spectrum Disorders*, 7(3), 455–465.

Mohiuddin, S. & Ghaziuddin, M. (2013). Psychopharmacology of autism spectrum disorders: a selective review. *Autism*, 17(6), 645–654. doi:10.1177/1362361312453776.

Muris, P., Steerneman, P., Merckelbach, H., Holdrinet, I., & Meesters, C. (1998). Comorbid anxiety symptoms in children with pervasive developmental disorders. *Journal of Anxiety Disorders*, 12(4), 387–393.

Pearson, D. A., Santos, C. W., Aman, M. G., Arnold, L. E., Casat, C. D., Mansour, R., et al. (2013). Effects of extended release methylphenidate treatment on ratings of attention-deficit/hyperactivity disorder (ADHD) and associated behavior in children with autism spectrum disorders and ADHD symptoms. *Journal of Child and Adolescent Psychopharmacology*, 23(5), 337–351. doi:10.1089/cap.2012.0096.

Rice, C. E., Zablotsky, B., Avila, R. M., Colpe, L. J., Schieve, L. A., Pringle, B., & Blumberg, S. J. (2016). Reported wandering behavior among children with autism spectrum disorder and/or intellectual disability. *Journal of Pediatrics*, 174, 232–239.

Rubenstein, L. D., Schelling, N., Wilczynski, S. M., & Hooks, E. N. (2015). Lived experiences of parents of gifted students with autism spectrum disorder. *Gifted Child Quarterly*, 59(4), 283–298. doi:10.1177/0016986215592193.

Salazar, F., Baird, G., Chandler, S., Tseng, E., O'Sullivan, T., Howlin, P., et al. (2015). Co-occurring psychiatric disorders in preschool and elementary school-aged children with autism spectrum disorder. *Journal of Autism & Developmental Disorders*, 45(8), 2283–2294.

Saulnier, C. A., & Ventola, P. E. (2012). *Essentials of Autism Spectrum Disorder Evaluation and Assessment*. Hoboken, NJ: Wiley.

Schieve, L. A., Gonzalez, V., Boulet, S. L., Visser, S. N., Rice, C. E., Van Naarden Braun, K., & Boyle, C. A. (2012). Concurrent medical conditions and health care use and needs among children with learning and behavioral developmental disabilities, National Health Interview Survey, 2006–2010. *Research in Developmental Disabilities*, 33(2), 467–476. doi:10.1016/j.ridd.2011.10.008.

Segers, M. & Rawana, J. (2014). What do we know about suicidality in autism spectrum disorders? A systematic review. *Autism Research*, 7(4), 507–521. doi:10.1002/aur.1375.

Sharp, W. G., Jaquess, D. L., Morton, J. F., & Herzinger, C. V. (2010). Pediatric feeding disorders: A quantitative synthesis of treatment outcomes. *Clinical Child & Family Psychology Review*, 13(4), 348–365. doi:10.1007/s10567-010-0079-7.

Sharp, W. G., Berry, R.C., McCracken, C., Nuhu, N. N., Marvel, E., Saulnier, C. A., et al. (2013). Feeding problems and nutrient intake in children with autism spectrum disorders: a meta-analysis and comprehensive review of the literature. *Journal of Autism and Developmental Disorders*, 43(9), 2159–2173. doi:10.1007/s10803-013-1771-5.

Soke, G. N., Maenner, M. J., Christensen, D., Kurzius-Spencer, M., & Schieve, L. A. (2018). Prevalence of co-occurring medical and behavioral conditions/symptoms among 4- and 8-year-old children with Autism Spectrum Disorder in selected areas of the United States in 2010. *Journal of Autism & Developmental Disorders*. doi:10.1007/s10803-018-3521-1.

Sparrow, S. S., Ciccheti, D. V., & Saulnier, C. A. (2016). *Vineland Adaptive Behavior Scales*, 3rd edn. San Antonio, TX: Pearson.

Spence, S. J. & Schneider, M. T. (2009). The role of epilepsy and epileptiform EEGs in autism spectrum disorders. *Pediatric Research*, 65(6), 599–606.

Sturman, N., Deckx, L., & van Driel, M. L. (2017). Methylphenidate for children and adolescents with autism spectrum disorder. *Cochrane Database Systematic Review*, 11, Cd011144. doi:10.1002/14651858.CD011144.pub2.

Sukhodolsky, D. G., Bloch, M. H., Panza, K. E., & Reichow, B. (2013). Cognitive-behavioral therapy for anxiety in children with high-functioning autism: a meta-analysis. *Pediatrics*, 132(5), e1341–1350. doi:10.1542/peds.2013-1193.

Taurines, R., Schwenck, C., Westerwald, E., Sachse, M., Siniatchkin, M., & Freitag, C. (2012). ADHD and autism: differential diagnosis or overlapping traits? A selective review. *Attention Deficit Hyperactive Disorder*, 4(3), 115–139. doi:10.1007/s12402-012-0086-2.

Thomas, S., Hovinga, M. E., Rai, D., & Lee, B. K. (2017). Brief report: Prevalence of co-occurring epilepsy and autism spectrum disorder: The U.S. national survey of children's health 2011–2012. *Journal of Autism & Developmental Disorders*, 47(1), 224–229. doi:10.1007/s10803-016-2938-7.

Tilford, J., Payakachat, N., Kuhlthau, K., Pyne, J., Kovacs, E., Bellando, J., et al. (2015). Treatment for sleep problems in children with autism and caregiver spillover effects. *Journal of Autism & Developmental Disorders*, 45(11), 3613–3623. doi:10.1007/s10803-015-2507-5.

White, S. W., Oswald, D., Ollendick, T., & Scahill, L. (2009). Anxiety in children and adolescents with autism spectrum disorders. *Clinical Psychology Review*, 29(3), 216–229. doi:10.1016/j.cpr.2009.01.003.

Wing, L. (1981). Asperger's syndrome: a clinical account. *Psychological Medicine*, 11, 115–129.

Worley, J. A., Matson, J. L., & Kozlowski, A. M. (2011). The effects of hearing impairment on symptoms of autism in toddlers. *Developmental Neurorehabilitation*, 14(3), 171–176. doi:10.3109/17518423.2011.564600.

Part II

Specific ASD Assessment Practices

Chapter 5

Primary Components of ASD Assessments

Although knowledge of neurobiological causes of autism spectrum disorders (ASD) has expanded over the last decade, there is no medical test for ASD. Its identification is based solely on observed behavioral symptomatology. Given the variability in the presentation of ASD, accurate identification can be difficult and requires experience with and knowledge of autism symptoms. Although there are many helpful assessment measures and tools, *the best tool in identifying ASD is the clinician's interpretation* of a child's history, current functioning, behavioral observations, and assessment results.

Screening for ASD

Autism identification in young children often begins when an ASD screener, designated to flag concerns about communication, social interaction, or repetitive or unusual behaviors, indicates concerns. Pediatricians may then refer families to their local school for additional evaluation. Although screeners are prevalent and extremely useful for flagging concerns, an ASD eligibility should never be made based solely on elevated scores on a screening measure. These scales can be elevated for a variety of reasons (i.e., social anxiety, behavioral disorder, intellectual disability) and a direct clinical assessment is necessary to consider differentials and determine if autism criteria are met. Many useful screeners exist, and some of the most commonly used include:

- *Modified Checklist for Autism in Toddlers* (Robins, Fein, & Barton, 1999);
- *Screening Tool for Autism in Two-Year-Olds* (Stone, Coonrod, & Ousley, 2000);
- *Communication and Symbolic Behavior Scales, Developmental Profile: Infant–Toddler Checklist* (Wetherby & Prizant, 2001).

Comprehensive ASD Assessment

Once a screening instrument indicates elevated scores, the next step is a comprehensive ASD assessment. Evaluators can include the following: School psychologist, clinical psychologist, pediatric neurologist, developmental pediatrician, or psychiatrist. Ideally a comprehensive assessment should be conducted by a multidisciplinary team that includes a school psychologist, a medical professional, and a speech and language pathologist. Occupational therapists and social workers also provide valuable information and guidance.

To help guide the diagnostic process, the National Autism Center (2015) outlined best practice guidelines for autism assessments in its National Standards Project Phase 2. These guidelines were developed by an expert panel of researchers and leaders in the field and were targeted at parents, caregivers, educators, and service providers. Although the primary goal was to provide information about which interventions have been shown to be effective, the project also outlined guidelines for appropriate and accurate autism identification. Best practice guidelines identify six essential components in a comprehensive diagnostic evaluation for autism (National Autism Center, 2015):

1. Parent or caregiver interview;
2. Review of records (including medical, psychological, and school records);
3. Cognitive or developmental assessment;
4. Direct play observation;
5. Measurement of adaptive functioning;
6. Comprehensive medical examination.

Parent Interview

A parent interview is essential to determine early developmental history and the extent to which the child is demonstrating symptoms in the home setting. Parent interviews are often conducted by a school psychologist or a school social worker. A good parent interview should include the following components: family history, social history, medical and birth history, detailed developmental history, current functioning, academic and service history, and previous testing results. Information about the child's environment and history of foster care is important because changes in early caretakers can affect a child's social interactions.

Although schools often give parents a questionnaire to complete, gathering additional ASD-specific information during an interview is more informative. Sometimes, this information can be gathered during or directly after a Response to Intervention meeting or Individualized

Example Parent/Caregiver Interview

Family History:
1. Family member's names, ages, living situation
2. Parent occupation and education level
3. History of trauma, abuse, or stressful events
4. Health, developmental, and psychiatric history of child's relatives; specifically, are there any relatives with ASD

Medical History:
1. Birth weight and perinatal/postnatal history
2. Maternal medications/substances used during pregnancy
3. History of illness/surgeries/hospitalizations
4. Current hearing and vision functioning
5. Current medications
6. Sleep patterns
7. Feeding patterns

Developmental and Behavioral History:
1. First Concerns:
   - How old was your child when you first had concerns?
   - What were you concerned about at that time?

2. Verbal Communication:
   - How old was your child when he/she first began using single words?
   - Was there ever a time when you child regressed?
   - When did he/she begin combining words into short phrases?
   - How does he/she communicate that he/she wants something?

   If verbal:
   - Does he/she ever use odd phrases or say the same thing over and over again?
   - Does he/she repeat words or phrases that he/she has heard from you or from television?
   - Does he/she get his/her pronouns mixed up (e.g. saying "you" instead of "I")
   - What kind of back and forth conversations can he/she have with you?
   - Do you notice anything about the tone of his/her voice?

3. Nonverbal Communication:
   - Gestures: Does he/she point to request? Does he/she nod to indicate yes; shake head to indicate no? Does he/she ever use other gestures to indicate what he/she wants?
   - Does he/she ever pull you by the hand to lead you to something?
   - Does he/she use your hand as tool?
   - How does he/she typically respond when you call his/her name?
   - Does he/she follow one-step instructions? Two step instructions?

4. Motor Skills
   - How old was he/she when he/she crawled? Walked independently?
   - Do you have current concerns about gross or fine motor skills?

5. Social Development:
   - Does he/she seem interested in other kids his/her age?
   - Does he/she try to join in with other kids?
   - Does he/she play imaginative games with another child? Describe.
   - How does he/she respond when other children approach him/her?
   - Does he/she spontaneously show you things to try to engage with you?
   - Does he/she offer to share things with you?
   - Does he/she look at you when doing things with you or talking with you?

   For school aged children:
   - Does he/she have any particular friends or best friend?

Figure 5.1 (continued)

(continued)

> 6. Interests/Activities/Play:
>   - What is your child interested in?
>   - What kinds of toys/objects does he/she like to play with? (probe for unusual fixations or interests that are unusual in their intensity)
>   - Does he/she ever seem to be more interested in parts of a toy (such as spinning the wheels) rather than playing with the whole toy?
>   - Does he/she have repetitive ways of playing (e.g. lining toys up)?
>
> 7. Behavior:
>   - When is he/she at his/her best? What time of day is it? What is he/she doing?
>   - Does your child have any behaviors that seem ritualized (e.g. needing to do things in a certain way or order)
>   - Does he/she become upset by small changes in his routine?
>   - Does he/she have any unusual or repetitive ways of moving his hands or fingers? Whole body?
>   - Does he/she ever hurt himself intentionally (e.g. banging his head, biting himself)?
>   - Does he/she ever try to hurt others (e.g. hitting, pushing, throwing objects at people)?
>   - What makes him/her upset? What does it look like? How often does it happen? How long does it take him/her to calm down?
>
> 8. Emotional (for school aged children):
>   - Is he/she often worried? What does he/she worry about?
>   - Is he/she often sad? What makes him/her sad?
>   - Does he/she hear or see things that other do not see?
>   - Has he/she ever threatened to hurt himself/herself?
>   - Has he/she ever threatened to hurt others?
>
> 9. Sensory:
>   - Does he/she seem interested in the sight, sound, taste, smell or feel of things or people?
>   - Is he/she particularly bothered by certain sounds, textures, tastes, or smells? How does he react to these things?
>
> 10. Adaptive:
>   - Is your child toilet trained for day and night? How old was he/she when toilet trained?
>   - Does your child feed himself/herself?
>   - Does your child dress himself/herself?
>   - Do you have any safety concerns related to wandering or other issues?
>
> **Intervention History:**
>   1. School history and repeated grades
>   2. Current special education eligibility and placement
>   3. Current private interventions
>   4. Previous private interventions
>   5. Previous psychiatric hospitalizations

Figure 5.1 Example parent/caregiver history

Education Program meeting. The historical information gathered in an interview can be critical in correctly identifying ASD.

The most common standardized parent interview is the revised version of the Autism Diagnostic Interview (Rutter, Bailey, & Lord 2003). This interview takes 90–150 minutes, including scoring, and is used primarily in research settings. In schools and clinical settings, there are often practical constraints that make it necessary to complete a parent interview more quickly.

Review of Records

A review of records is an essential component of a thorough assessment for several reasons. It is often difficult for parents to remember details of their child's development and history. Furthermore, a good review of records offers insight into the child's functioning across multiple settings. Records from early intervention programing or preschool can be helpful in identifying the child's social communication and interaction early on. Records can also offer important insight into possible progress or regression over time.

When reviewing records in a Response to Intervention meeting, standardized test scores may provide clues that the team should be considering a possible ASD. Specifically, splits between verbal and nonverbal cognitive abilities may be present. At the point of determining special education eligibility, a review of report cards can also provide information about a child's educational functioning. Although a child may be performing adequately academically, he or she may show weaknesses in learning behaviors (e.g., completes works, cooperates in group work, listens appropriately) on the report card. This can signify an educational impact of ASD.

Cognitive or Developmental Measures

A standardized measure of development or cognition is important in the initial identification of ASD for several reasons. First, it is important to establish a child's level of functioning, so that his or her social interaction and communication skills can be evaluated in the context of his or her overall developmental or cognitive profile. A cognitive measure also helps to determine specific strengths and weaknesses within a child's profile. In many cases, children with autism demonstrate stronger nonverbal reasoning skills compared with their verbal skills, or may demonstrate significant variability across a variety of tasks. Many factors should be taken into account when choosing a measure to assess level of functioning.

Toddlers and Preschool Students

Considerations should include a child's ability to understand and attend to verbal instructions, the level of structure needed to elicit a child's optimal performance, and the degree to which social difficulties may interfere with the child's performance. Furthermore, measures should be chosen based on a child's level of functioning, rather than his or her age. Common measures of development and early cognitive ability include:

- *Bayley Scales of Infant and Toddler Development*, 3rd edn (Bayley, 2006);
- *Mullen Scales of Early Learning* (Mullen, 1995);
- *Differential Ability Scale*, 2nd edn (Elliot, 2007);
- *Wechsler Preschool and Primary Scales of Intelligence*, 4th edn (Wechsler, 2012);
- *Stanford–Binet Intelligence Scales*, 5th edn (Roid, 2003).

Although each of these tests can provide important data about a child's level of functioning, certain tests have particular strengths for use with this population. For example, the Differential Ability Scales, 2nd edn (DAS-II: Elliott, 2007) is useful with preschool-age children with ASD, because of the lower verbal demands of some tasks, appealing manipulatives, and the fact that the core battery can be administered in 25–40 minutes. Another benefit of the DAS-II is the inclusion of teaching items in which the examiner models completion of the task over several items. This is particularly helpful for children who struggle with verbal comprehension. The Stanford–Binet is helpful in that it provides norms for ages 2.5 to 85; this broad age range can be particularly useful for children who have significant delays in some areas, but average to above-average scores in others. Both the Bayley Scales of Infant and Toddler Development, 3rd edn and the Mullen Scales of Early Learning are useful with younger preschoolers and toddlers.

Patterns of scores on cognitive/developmental tests can be indicative of ASD. First, in children with ASD, their verbal abilities are often significantly lower than their nonverbal abilities (Maljaars et al., 2012; Nowell et al., 2015). Therefore, selecting a cognitive measure that separates verbal and nonverbal cognitive abilities is important. A second pattern is related to their verbal language abilities. Children often demonstrate stronger expressive language skills than receptive language skills (Hudry et al., 2010; Volden et al., 2011). So, they may perform well on a picture-naming vocabulary subtest but struggle with a subtest that requires following directions (e.g., "Give me the cow").

School-age Students

Children who are functioning at a school-age level can be given a cognitive measure. This can yield important information about a child's strengths and weaknesses, and identify specific processing deficits or learning difficulties. For children on the autism spectrum, challenges often emerge about age 8 as children transition from rote concrete learning to more conceptual and abstract learning (e.g., reading to learn rather than learning to read). Children with ASD tend to struggle with this more conceptual learning. Cognitive measures that are commonly used include:

- *Differential Ability Scales*, 2nd edn (Elliott, 2007);
- *Wechsler Intelligence Scale for Children*, 5th edn (Wechsler, 2014);
- *Stanford–Binet Intelligence Scales*, 5th edn (Roid, 2003);
- *Woodcock Johnson Test of Cognitive Abilities*, 4th edn (Schrank et al., 2014);
- *Kaufman Assessment Battery for Children*, 2nd edn (Kaufman & Kaufman, 2004).

It is also important to have familiarity with nonverbal cognitive measures for those students who are minimally verbal. Nonverbal measures can also be beneficial for children who are bilingual because they reduce verbal language demands. Common nonverbal intelligence measures include:

- *Comprehensive Test of Nonverbal Intelligence*, 2nd edn (Hammill, Pearson, & Weiderholt, 2009);
- *Leiter International Performance Scale*, 3rd edn (Pomplun & Koch, 2013);
- *Universal Nonverbal Intelligence Test*, 2nd edn (Bracken & McCallum, 2016).

Although each child with ASD presents with his or her own unique profile, certain patterns tend to emerge with frequency. Discrepancies between verbal and nonverbal abilities are common in school-age children with ASD. Estimates suggest that approximately 30–40% will demonstrate significant discrepancies between their verbal and nonverbal abilities (Nowell et al., 2015). Similar to findings with young children, school-age children are more likely to show a strength in nonverbal cognitive abilities compared with verbal abilities (Matthews et al., 2015). However, within school-age children, it is also common for children to show a strength in verbal cognitive abilities compared with nonverbal abilities (Nowell et al., 2015).

Some subtests also tend to show patterns of strengths and weaknesses. On the Wechsler Intelligence Scale for Children, 5th edn, within the Verbal Comprehension domain, Comprehension is often significantly lower than Vocabulary and Similarities Scores (Mayes & Calhoun, 2008). In addition, Similarities and Matrices can be relative strengths (Mayes & Calhoun, 2008; Mouga et al., 2016; Oliveras-Rentas et al., 2012).

Direct Play Observation/Assessment

The goal of the direct play observation is to create a naturalistic, playful context through which the core symptoms of ASD can be assessed in a systematic way. A good play observation relies heavily on the clinician's own clinical judgment, knowledge of typical development, and expertise in symptoms of ASD. Observations during natural settings that

> **Play-based Assessment Observation**
>
> - What is the child's verbal repertoire?
> - Is the child able to use his/her verbal language in flexible ways to communicate with others?
> - What strategies does a child use to make requests?
> - Are there any atypical speech patterns such as pronoun reversal, echolalia or scripted speech?
> - Can the child participate in a back and forth conversation?
> - Can the child respond to open ended questions?
> - What nonverbal communication strategies are being used? (e.g. gestures, pointing)
> - Does the child respond to his/her name?
> - Does the child integrate eye contact with his/her other nonverbal and verbal communication strategies?
> - What is the frequency of social overtures to others such as showing, giving, and initiating joint attention
> - Does the child shift his/her gaze from objects of interest to people?
> - Does the child respond to the social overtures of others?
> - What does the child's play look like? Is it mostly cause -and-effect, functional play, or symbolic play? Are they able to engage in complex imaginative play with others?
> - Are there repetitive behaviors such as hand flapping?
> - Are there highly restricted interests such as letters/numbers, cars, or string?
> - Are unusual sensory interests present such as prolonged visual inspection of the wheels on cars or the feeling certain textures?
> - How is the child's behavior different with and without structure?
> - Can the child both take the lead in play and follow others?
> - Does the child transition between activities well?

Figure 5.2 Play-based assessment observation

encourage social interactions such as the playground, lunchroom, and special activities (e.g., art, physical education) can be particularly helpful. During a play assessment the clinician needs to create opportunities for communication and interaction, while simultaneously observing the child's skills and behaviors, and conceptualizing whether the behaviors fall into the pattern of a primary social communication disability.

Autism Diagnostic Observation Schedule, 2nd edn (ADOS-2)

Given the difficulty of assessing this broad range of behaviors while simultaneously interacting with the child, the use of a semi-structured play assessment is highly recommended (Figure 5.2). The Autism Diagnostic Observation Schedule, 2nd edn (ADOS-2; Lord et al., 2012) is considered to be the gold standard for direct assessment of autism symptomatology; it allows the examiner to probe for specific social and communication vulnerabilities during play and interview-based activities. It should be noted that the ADOS-2 does require extensive training in order to administer, score, and interpret. The ADOS-2 offers five modules, which are chosen based on the child's age and language level. The five modules are described below:

1   Toddler module: For children ages 12–30 months who are walking, have a nonverbal mental age of 12 months or more, and are pre-verbal or have single word speech;
2   Module 1: For children over the age of 30 months who are pre-verbal or have single-word speech;
3   Module 2: For children who have spontaneous phrase speech;
4   Module 3: For children who have fluent speech (i.e., can speak about non-present events and use sentences with multiple clauses);
5   Module 4: For children with fluent speech who are at a developmental level of 14 years or more.

It should be noted that, even with a "gold standard" tool such as the ADOS-2, a clinician needs to interpret the scores within context. A high score does not necessarily mean that the child has an ASD. For example, children with emotional and behavioral problems but not ASD may have high ADOS-2 scores (Havdahl et al., 2016; Molloy et al., 2011).

Childhood Autism Rating Scale, 2nd edn (CARS-2)

Although the ADOS-2 is an excellent tool, it may not always be needed or feasible to use in an assessment. At times, ASD symptoms are clear and a more time-efficient direct measure may be appropriate. The Childhood Autism Rating Scale, 2nd edn (CARS-2: Schopler et al., 2010) is one such measure. It is a clinician-completed rating based on direct behavioral observations and parent report. Two versions of the form are available, namely the Standard Form, for young children and older children with communication and/or cognitive weaknesses, and the High Functioning Form, for children over the age of 6 who are verbally fluent and have average cognitive abilities. Studies have shown that the previous edition of CARS was able to accurately distinguish children with ASD from those who do not have ASD; however, it tended to slightly underestimate ASD symptoms (Chlebowski et al., 2010). Both versions of the CARS-2 have high levels of sensitivity (i.e., ability to accurately identify children who do not have ASD) and specificity (i.e., ability to accurately identify children who have ASD; Dawkins, Meyer, & Van Bourgondien, 2016).

Monterio Interview Guidelines for Diagnosing the Autism Spectrum, 2nd edn (MIGDAS-2)

The Monterio Interview Guidelines for Diagnosing the Autism Spectrum (MIGDAS-2: Monteiro & Stegall, 2018) includes information gathered from parents and teachers as well as a sensory-based interview with the child. The interview with parents and teachers gathers information related to sensory use and interests, language and communication, and social relationships and emotional responses. The MIGDAS-2 results in a child's unique behavioral profile.

Adaptive Functioning

A good assessment of adaptive skills is a key component of a comprehensive autism evaluation. Adaptive behavior is generally defined as performance of skills that are necessary for personal and social sufficiency (Sparrow, Cicchetti, & Balla, 2005). These are skills an individual performs, independently, in daily activities, not just skills they are capable of performing when at their very best. An adaptive impairment exists when an individual is capable of performing a skill but does not independently do so. For example, if a child is capable of using the word "more" but does not do so spontaneously to make requests, this would be a deficit in adaptive communication.

Adaptive delays are often seen in children with ASD, and are often more pronounced than delays in cognitive skills. In fact, research has shown that adaptive impairments continue to be a significant problem for many children with ASD, even as they make important gains in their conceptual development (Klin et al., 2007). Therefore, the gap between cognitive and adaptive skills may increase over time.

Adaptive behaviors are typically assessed via parent and teacher reports because it is important to gain an understanding of the skills a child is spontaneously demonstrating in his or her home and school environments. These measures can be administered via a clinician interview with the parent or parent and teacher report forms. When time allows, direct interviews are recommended, so that the distinction between "can perform" and "does perform" can be differentiated throughout the interview by the clinician. Common measures of adaptive functioning include:

- *Vineland Adaptive Behavior Scales*, 3rd edn (Sparrow et al., 2016);
- *Adaptive Behavior Assessment System*, 3rd edn (Harrison & Oakland, 2015);
- *Scales of Independent Behavior*, revised (Bruininks et al., 2006).

There are specific patterns within adaptive functioning that can be indicative of an ASD. Although adaptive skills are often weaker than cognitive abilities, this gap between adaptive and cognitive abilities often increases over time (Kanne et al., 2011; Matthews et al., 2015). Patterns may also be apparent between scales on an adaptive measure. For example, on the Vineland-II and ABAS-2 the social domain is often a relative weakness (Doobay et al., 2014; Kanne et al., 2011; Kenworthy et al., 2010; Matthews et al., 2015). For children that have a particular interest in letters and numbers, there may also be stronger written skills than expressive and receptive language on Vineland measures.

Case Study 1

Jonathan is a 4-year-old boy who presented with behavioral concerns. His parents described that he was rigid and had meltdowns when schedules changed or he could not have access to his preferred items. He demonstrated a strong interest in in shapes and numbers. During cognitive testing, he was well regulated, and showed sustained interest and attention to tasks.

Differential Ability Scale, 2nd edn – DAS-II, Upper Early Years: Nonverbal Reasoning: 93 (Picture Similarities: 49; Matrices: 44); Spatial: 92 (Pattern Construction: 50; Copying: 41); Verbal: 83 (Verbal Comprehension: 31; Naming Vocabulary: 43).

Vineland Adaptive Behavior Scales, 3rd edn, Survey Interview: Communication: 97 (Receptive: 12; Expressive: 13; Written: 19); Daily Living Skills: 87 (Personal: 11; Domestic: 14; Community: 14); Socialization: 77 (Interpersonal Relationships: 12; Play and Leisure Time: 10; Coping Skills: 11); Motor: 64 (Gross Motor: 12; Fine Motor: 6).

Autism Diagnostic Observation Schedule – 2, Module 2: Comparison Score 4.

What patterns are present on the DAS-2 that are indicative of an ASD?

What patterns are present on the Vineland-3 that are indicative of an ASD?

Rating Scales

Rating scales can be useful for assessing a child's social skills and behaviors associated with ASD. They are considered more appropriate for screening than diagnostic level interpretation. Most rating scales have parent and teacher report versions so that behavioral information can be obtained across multiple settings. Examiners are encouraged to carefully examine the norm sample as well as reliability and validity of the measures. Commonly used ASD-specific rating scales include:

- *Social Communication Questionnaire* (Rutter, 2003);
- *Social Responsiveness Scale*, 2nd edn (Constantino & Gruber, 2012);
- *Autism Spectrum Rating Scale* (Goldstein & Naglieri, 2013).

For ASD-specific rating scales, the Social Communication Questionnaire and Social Responsiveness Scale have shown good sensitivity and specificity (Hampton & Strand, 2015; Norris & Lecavalier, 2010).

An important caution is that rating scales should never be used in isolation to determine an ASD eligibility. Some scales include interpretations that symptoms fall in the "autism range," but this finding is not sufficient to determine the child's eligibility. Elevated scores on a rating scale are quite useful; however, ratings can be elevated for a number reasons other than true ASD symptoms. For example, a child with an emotional or behavioral problem or an intellectual disability might have elevated scores (Havdahl et al., 2016). Also, it is important to remember that rating scales are subjective measures and do not directly measure a child's behavior. Elevated rating scales offer a compelling reason to complete a full comprehensive assessment so that the underlying cause of those behavioral difficulties can be better understood.

Broad-based rating scales can be helpful in considering differential or comorbid conditions. For example, a broad rating scale may suggest that a child has an anxiety problem rather than an ASD. Alternatively, it could indicate that a child has significant aggressive behaviors that are comorbid with ASD. Board-based rating scales include:

- *Behavior Assessment System for Children* (BASC), 3rd edn (Reynolds & Kamphaus, 2015);
- *Conners Early Childhood Scale* (Conners, 2009);
- *Achenbach System of Empirically Based Assessment* (Achenbach, 2009);

Although these broad scales are not specific to ASD, several of their scales are sensitive to ASD. The Withdrawn and Pervasive Developmental Problems scales on Child Behavior Checklist for Children, ages 1.5–5 years effectively screen for ASD (Norris & Lecavalier, 2010; Predescu et al., 2013). On the BASC, the Atypicality, Withdrawal, Developmental Social Disorders scales tend to be elevated in children with ASD (Lopata et al., 2016; Volker et al., 2010). Figure 5.3 summarizes some of the clues that a child has an ASD.

The determination of whether or not a child meets criteria for ASD can be difficult. The following are some patterns to look for in the data and helpful hints. They do not have to be present for a child to have an ASD, but they can indicate symptoms of ASD.

- Is there a verbal versus nonverbal cognitive split?
- Are there lower scores in receptive versus expressive communication skills?
- Are adaptive scores weaker than cognitive abilities?
- Are adaptive scores in the areas of communication and social skills particularly weak?
- Reread the developmental history. Was there a history of early language delays? What about feeding or sleeping problems?

Figure 5.3 Clues that a child has an ASD

Medical Evaluation

Another important component of a comprehensive autism evaluation is a thorough medical examination. There are many reasons for this. First, it is important to rule out possible medical causes for observed symptomatology. Hearing and vision should always be checked, because certain symptoms are better explained by these impairments. For example, a child who is hard of hearing may not respond to her name, and a child with visual impairment may hold items close to his eyes in a way that mimics peering or visual inspection.

In addition to ruling out possible medical explanations for symptoms, a medical evaluation can help to determine the etiology of the autism symptoms. Our understanding of the role of genetics in ASD has advanced considerably, therefore, the medical evaluation plays an important role in determining what genetic tests should be ordered for each child based on his or her symptom presentation and physical exam.

Other medical tests may also be deemed necessary based on the child's history and physical examination. For example, an electroencephalogram (EEG) may be recommended for a child who has a history of seizures, acute developmental regression, or unexplained behavioral change. MRI may be recommended for children with acute regression, microcephaly, or other abnormalities on neurological examination. Given the impact that neurological, metabolic, or other medical problems can have on a child's ability to benefit from intervention, referral to a physician is critical for children who are diagnosed with ASD in a non-medical setting such as school. After receiving a diagnosis in a non-medical setting, parents should be encouraged to share the evaluation report with the child's pediatrician.

Speech and Language Assessment

Although the National Standards Project (2015) did not specifically identify a speech and language assessment as a necessary component of an initial diagnostic evaluation, it does maintain that speech and language assessment and therapy is one of the first and most important steps in providing intervention for children with ASD. Thus, whenever possible, a thorough language evaluation should be included for children presenting with symptoms of ASD. In addition, many states require a speech and language evaluation in determining ASD eligibility.

Speech and language evaluations assess receptive language, expressive language, conversational skills (e.g., topic management, turn-taking), speech prosody (e.g., speech stress, tone, rhythm), and social communication.

A core feature of ASD is impairment and social or pragmatic communication. Although many children with ASD are capable of producing verbal language, they often struggle with the social use of language such as paying attention to nonverbal cues, using eye contact and appropriate body language, turn-taking in conversation, listening, understanding non-literal language, and responding to humor. Thus, a thorough assessment of pragmatic language is particularly important in establishing the eligibility and also to determine areas of weakness to be targeted through intervention programing.

In addition to formal tests, language samples can gather representative samples of a child's speech. These are particularly important in assessing pragmatic language because children with ASD can sometimes perform better on structured formal assessments than in more naturalistic language samples. In order to assess language, speech and language pathologists may use:

- *Clinical Evaluation of Language Fundamentals*, 5th edn (Wiig, Semel, & Secord, 2013);
- *Comprehensive Assessment of Spoken Language* (Corrow-Woolfolk, 1999);
- *Preschool Language Scale*, 5th edn (Zimmerman, Steiner, & Pond, 2011);
- *Test of Pragmatic Language*, 2nd edn (Phelps-Terasaki & Phelps-Gunn, 2007);
- *Children's Communication Checklist*, 2nd edn (Bishop, 2006).

References

Achenbach, T. M. (2009). *Achenbach System of Empirically Based Assessment (ASEBA): Development, findings, theory, and applications*. Burlington, VT: University of Vermont, Research Center of Children, Youth & Families.

Bayley, N. (2005). *Bayley Scales of Infant and Toddler Development*, 3rd edn. San Antonio, TX: Harcourt Assessment.

Bishop, D. (2006). *Children's Communication Checklist 2*, US edn. San Antonio, TX: Harcourt Assessment.

Bracken, B. A, & McCallum, R. S. (2016). *Universal Nonverbal Intelligence Test*, 2nd edn. Austin, TX: PRO-ED.

Bruininks, R. H., Woodcock, R. W., Weatherman, R. F., Hill, B. K., Strauss, E., Sherman, E. M. S., & Spreen, O. (2006). *Scales of Independent Behavior*, revised. New York: Oxford University Press.

Chlebowski, C., Green, J. A., Barton, M. L., & Fein, D. (2010). Using the childhood autism rating scale to diagnose autism spectrum disorders. *Journal of Autism & Developmental Disorders*, 40(7), 787–799. doi:10.1007/s10803-009-0926-x.

Conners, C. K. (2009). *Conners Early Childhood*. Toronto, Ontario, Canada: Multi-Health Systems.

Constantino, J. N., & Gruber, C. P. (2012). *Social Responsiveness Scale*, 2nd edn. Torrance, CA: Western Psychological Services.

Carrow-Woolfolk, E. (1999). *Comprehensive Assessment of Spoken Language*. Bloomington, MN: Pearson.

Dawkins, T., Meyer, A. T., & Van Bourgondien, M. E. (2016). The relationship between the Childhood Autism Rating Scale: Second Edition and clinical diagnosis utilizing the DSM-IV-TR and the DSM-5. *Journal of Autism & Developmental Disorders*, 46(10), 3361–3368. doi:10.1007/s10803-016-2860-z.

Doobay, A., Foley-Nicpon, M., Ali, S., & Assouline, S. (2014). Cognitive, adaptive, and psychosocial differences between high ability youth with and without autism spectrum disorder. *Journal of Autism & Developmental Disorders*, 44(8), 2026–2040. doi:10.1007/s10803-014-2082-1.

Elliot, C. D. (2007). *Differential Ability Scales*, 2nd edn. San Antonio, TX: Harcourt.

Goldstein, S. & Naglieri, J. A. (2013). *Autism Spectrum Rating Scales*. East Aurora, NY: Slosson Educational Publications.

Hammill, D. D., Pearson, N. A., & Weiderholt, J. L. (2009). *Comprehensive Test of Nonverbal Intelligence*, 2nd edn. Austin, TX: PRO-ED.

Hampton, J., & Strand, P. (2015). A review of level 2 parent-report instruments used to screen children aged 1.5-5 for autism: A meta-analytic update. *Journal of Autism & Developmental Disorders*, 45(8), 2519–2530. doi:10.1007/s10803-015-2419-4.

Harrison, P. L. & Oakland, T. (2015). *Adaptive Behavior Assessment System*, 3rd edn. Bloomington, MN: Pearson.

Havdahl, K. A., Hus Bal, V., Huerta, M., Pickles, A., Oyen, A. S., Stoltenberg, C., et al. (2016). Multidimensional influences on autism symptom measures: Implications for use in etiological research. *Journal of American Academic Child & Adolescent Psychiatry*, 55(12), 1054–1063. e1053. doi:10.1016/j.jaac.2016.09.490.

Hudry, K., Leadbitter, K., Temple, K., Slonims, V., McConachie, H., Aldred, C., et al. (2010). Preschoolers with autism show greater impairment in receptive compared with expressive language abilities. *International Journal of Language & Communication Disorders*, 45(6), 681–690. doi:10.3109/13682820903461493.

Kanne, S. M., Gerber, A. J., Quirmbach, L. N., Sparrow, S. S., Cicchetti, D. V., & Saulnier, C. A. (2011). The role of adaptive behavior in autism spectrum disorders: Implications for functional outcome. *Journal of Autism & Developmental Disorders*, 41(8), 1007–1018. doi:10.1007/s10803-010-1126-4.

Kaufman, A. S. & Kaufman, N. L. (2004). *Kaufman Assessment Battery for Children*, 2nd edn. Circle Pines, MN: American Guidance Service.

Kenworthy, L., Case, L., Harms, M. B., Martin, A., & Wallace, G. L. (2010). Adaptive behavior ratings correlate with symptomatology and IQ among individuals with high-functioning autism spectrum disorders. *Journal of Autism & Developmental Disorders*, 40(4), 416–423. doi:10.1007/s10803-009-0911-4.

Klin, A., Saulnier, C. A., Sparrow, S. S., Cicchetti, D. V., Volkmar, F. R., & Lord, C. (2007). Social and communication abilities and disabilities in higher functioning individuals with autism spectrum disorders: The Vineland and the ADOS. *Journal of Autism and Developmental Disorders*, 37(4), 748–759. doi:10.1007/s10803-006-0229-4.

Lopata, C., Donnelly, J. P., Jordan, A. K., Thomeer, M. L., McDonald, C. A., & Rodgers, J. D. (2016). Brief report: Parent–teacher discrepancies on the developmental Social Disorders Scale (BASC-2) in the assessment of high-functioning children with ASD. *Journal of Autism & Developmental Disorders*, 46(9), 3183–3189. doi:10.1007/s10803-016-2851-0.

Lord, C., Luyster, R. J., Gotham, K., & Guthrie, W. (2012). *Autism Diagnostic Observation Schedule*, 2nd edn. Torrance, CA: Western Psychological Services.

Maljaars, J., Noens, I., Scholte, E., & Berckelaer-Onnes, I. (2012). Language in low-functioning children with autistic disorder: Differences between receptive and expressive skills and concurrent predictors of language. *Journal of Autism & Developmental Disorders*, 42(10), 2181–2191. doi:10.1007/s10803-012-1476-1.

Matthews, N., Pollard, E., Ober-Reynolds, S., Kirwan, J., Malligo, A., & Smith, C. (2015). Revisiting cognitive and adaptive functioning in children and adolescents with autism spectrum disorder. *Journal of Autism & Developmental Disorders*, 45(1), 138–156. doi:10.1007/s10803-014-2200-0.

Mayes, S. D. & Calhoun, S. L. (2008). WISC-IV and WIAT-II profiles in children with high-functioning autism. *Journal of Autism & Developmental Disorders*, 38(3), 428–439. doi:10.1007/s10803-007-0410-4.

Molloy, C. A., Murray, D. S., Akers, R., Mitchell, T., & Manning-Courtney, P. (2011). Use of the Autism Diagnostic Observation Schedule (ADOS) in a clinical setting. *Autism*, 15(2), 143–162. doi:10.1177/1362361310379241.

Monteiro, M. J. & Stegall, S. (2018). *Monteiro Interview Guidelines for Diagnosing the Autism Spectrum – 2*. Los Angeles, CA: Western Psychological Services.

Mouga, S., Cafe, C., Almeida, J., Marques, C., Duque, F., & Oliveira, G. (2016). Intellectual profiles in the Autism Spectrum and other neurodevelopmental disorders. *Journal of Autism & Developmental Disorders*, 46(9), 2940–2955. doi:10.1007/s10803-016-2838-x.

Mullen, E. (1995). *Mullen Scales of Early Learning*. Circle Pines, MN: American Guidance Service.

National Autism Center (2015). *Findings and Conclusions: National standards project, Phase 2*. Randolph, MN: National Autism Center.

Norris, M. & Lecavalier, L. (2010). Screening accuracy of level 2 autism spectrum disorder rating scales. *Autism: International Journal of Research & Practice*, 14(4), 263–284. doi:10.1177/1362361309348071.

Nowell, K., Schanding, G., Kanne, S., & Goin-Kochel, R. (2015). Cognitive profiles in youth with autism spectrum disorder: An investigation of base rate discrepancies using the Differential Ability Scales, 2nd edn. *Journal of Autism & Developmental Disorders*, 45(7), 1978–1988. doi:10.1007/s10803-014-2356-7.

Oliveras-Rentas, R. E., Kenworthy, L., Roberson, R. B., 3rd, Martin, A., & Wallace, G. L. (2012). WISC-IV profile in high-functioning autism spectrum disorders: impaired processing speed is associated with increased autism communication symptoms and decreased adaptive communication abilities. *Journal of Autism & Developmental Disorders*, 42(5), 655–664. doi:10.1007/s10803-011-1289-7.

Phelps-Terasaki, D. & Phelps-Gunn, T. (2007). *Test of Pragmatic Language*, 2nd edn. Austin, TX: Pro-Ed Publishing.
Pomplun, M. & Koch, C. (2013). *Leiter International Performance Scale*, 3rd edn. Torrance, CA: Western Psychological Services.
Predescu, E., ŞIpos, R., Dobrean, A., & MicluȚIa, I. (2013). The discriminative power of the CBCL 1.5-5 between autism spectrum disorders and other psychiatric disorders. *Journal of Cognitive & Behavioral Psychotherapies*, 13(1), 75–87.
Reynolds, C. R. & Kamphaus, R. W. (2015). *Behavior Assessment System for Children*, 3rd edn. San Antonio, TX: Pearson.
Robins, D. L., Fein, D., & Barton, M. (1999). *The Modified Checklist for Autism in Toddlers* (M-CHAT). Self-published.
Roid, G. H. (2003). *Stanford–Binet Intelligence Scales*, 5th edn. Torrance, CA: Western Psychological Services.
Rutter, M., Bailey, A., & Lord, C. (2003). *Social Communication Questionnaire*. Torrance, CA: Western Psychological Services.
Schopler, E., Van Bourgondien, M. E., Wellman, G. J., & Love, S. R. (2010). *Childhood Autism Rating Scale*, 2nd edn. Torrance, CA: Western Psychological Services.
Schrank, F. A., McGrew, K. S., Mather, N., & Woodcock, R. W. (2014). *Woodcock–Johnson IV Tests of Cognitive Abilities*. Rolling Meadows, IL: Riverside Publishing.
Sparrow, S. S., Ciccheti, D. V., & Saulnier, C. A. (2016). *Vineland Adaptive Behavior Scales*, 3rd edn. San Antonio, TX: Pearson.
Stone, W., Coonrod, E. E., & Ousley, OY. (2000). Brief report: screening tool for autism in two-year-olds (STAT): development and preliminary data. *Journal of Autism & Developmental Disorders*, 30(6), 607–612.
Volden, J., Smith, I. M., Szatmari, P., Bryson, S., Fombonne, E., Mirenda, P., et al. (2011). Using the Preschool Language Scale, Fourth Edition to characterize language in preschoolers with autism spectrum disorders. *American Journal of Speech–Language Pathology*, 20(3), 200–208. doi:10.1044/1058-0360(2011/10-0035).
Volker, M. A., Lopata, C., Smerbeck, A. M., Knoll, V. A., Thomeer, M. L., Toomey, J. A., & Rodgers, J. D. (2010). BASC-2 PRS profiles for students with high-functioning autism spectrum disorders. *Journal of Autism & Developmental Disorders*, 40(2), 188–199. doi:10.1007/s10803-009-0849-6.
Wechsler, D. (2012). *Wechsler Preschool and Primary Scale of Intelligence*, 4th edn. Bloomington, MN: Pearson.
Wechsler, D. (2014). *Wechsler Intelligence Scale for Children*, 5th edn. In: N. Benson & Keith, T. Z. (eds), *WISC-V*. Bloomington, MN: Pearson.
Wetherby, A. & Prizant, B. (2001). *Communication and Symbolic Behavior Scales Developmental Profile Infant/Toddler Checklist*. Baltimore, MD: Brookes Publishing.
Wiig, E. H., Semel, E., & Secord, W. A. (2013). *Clinical Evaluation of Language Fundamentals*, 5th edn. San Antonio, TX: Pearson.
Zimmerman, I. L., Steiner, V. G., & Pond, R. E. (2011). *Preschool Language Scales*, 5th edn. Bloomington, MN: Pearson/PsychCorp.

Chapter 6

Secondary Components of ASD Assessments

Although the core components of an ASD evaluation are a caregiver interview, review of records, cognitive assessment, direct play observation, speech and language evaluation, measurement of adaptive functioning, and medical examination, additional information is helpful for the purposes of a school-based assessment. Schools are tasked with teaching academic skills; therefore, assessment of children's reading, writing, and math skills, and their underlying psychological processes are valued in an ASD assessment. Just as there is heterogeneity in the presentation of children with autism spectrum disorders (ASD), there is also no one learning profile for children with ASD. The academic profiles of children with ASD as well as their psychological processing abilities vary significantly. However, understanding a child's unique academic and psychological processing profile can direct intervention efforts. Children with ASD can demonstrate particular academic strengths just as much as they might demonstrate particular academic weaknesses.

Similar to the general population, overall cognitive abilities of children with ASD, as represented by a full-scale cognitive measure, are predictive of academic abilities (Keen, Webster, & Ridley, 2016; Miller et al., 2017). Children with ASD and lower cognitive abilities (full-scale intelligence quotient [FSIQ] <70) tend to have weaker academic skills than peers with ASD and average cognitive abilities (FSIQ ≥70; Keen et al., 2016). However, for individual children with average cognitive abilities there are often discrepancies between their actual academic achievement and their expected academic achievement based on cognitive abilities, with some achieving higher and others lower than expected (Estes et al., 2011). Overall, many children will achieve academic skills consistent with or stronger than their cognitive abilities, but there is a substantial number who demonstrate particularly weak academic skills in at least one area (Kim, Bal, & Lord, 2017). Therefore, screening for academic problems is particularly important for children with ASD. In other words, children with ASD are more likely than their typically developing peers to have personal academic strengths and weaknesses (Figure 6.1).

> - Exceptional letter identification, word reading skills, and spelling skills.
> - Exceptional number identification or math computation skills.
> - Difficulties with concepts of print in young children.
> - Preference and strength in reading nonfiction versus fictional texts.
> - Weaknesses in more applied, abstract academic skills in reading comprehension, math reasoning, and written expression.

Figure 6.1 Possible academic patterns in children with ASD

Several factors are associated with general academic performance. Children with more severe symptoms of ASD as measured by tools such as the CARS have weaker academic skills (Miller et al., 2017). In contrast, the problem behavior of children with ASD has not been shown to be associated with academic achievement (Estes et al., 2011). A small group of children who are identified as having ASD when they are very young show optimal outcomes and no longer meet ASD criteria when they reach adolescence. In fact, they show similar academic patterns of performance as their typically developing peers (Troyb et al., 2014a).

In general, the literature on the academic skills of children with ASD is limited and what exists focuses on children with average to above-average cognitive abilities. There is very little information about the academic growth of students with cognitive ability standard scores <70. For these children, goals focus more on functional than on academic skills. In addition, they may be taking alternate assessments that are not as easily used in research. Therefore, most of the information presented in this chapter refers to children with ASD and cognitive ability standard scores >70.

Assessing Academic Skills and Psychological Processing

A number of broad-band achievement measures can be used to measure children with ASD's academic reading, writing, and math skills. Academic assessment measures include:

- *Kaufman Test of Educational Achievement* – 3rd edn (Kaufman & Kaufman, 2014);
- *Wechsler Individual Achievement Test* – 3rd edn (Wechsler, 2009);
- *Woodcock Johnson IV Tests of Achievement* (Schrank et al., 2014a).

There is not one test that is clearly preferable over the others. In considering an assessment battery, school psychologists should consider the student's unique academic profile in order to fully capture the student's academic strengths and weaknesses. For example, when measuring reading

Table 6.1 Psychological processes

- Executive functioning
- Long-term retrieval
- Nonverbal/Fluid reasoning
- Phonological processing
- Processing speed
- Verbal/Crystallized reasoning
- Visual–spatial–orthographic processing
- Working memory

comprehension, it is helpful to use a subtest that uses fiction and nonfiction passages, because fiction passages may be more difficult. In addition, subtests that measure children's skills in answering inferential and predictive questions about passages may be beneficial because these are also more challenging. When assessing math abilities, ensuring that measures of math problem-solving are included in addition to math calculation are used will illuminate important differences. Finally, when assessing writing, more naturalistic assessment measures that require a student to compose a paragraph or essay are informative. If a student is required only to respond to prompts with single sentences, opportunities to assess weaknesses in writing caused by executive functioning and working memory are decreased.

In assessing children with ASD's psychological processing (Table 6.1), it is important to assess major areas of processing as outlined by the Cattell–Horn–Carroll theory. In particular, assessing processing areas that are associated with the child's area of academic weakness is beneficial. For example, for a child with basic reading problems, assessing their phonological processing and rapid automatic naming are of particular importance.

Again, there are a number of appropriate assessments available. Broad cognitive assessments that assess psychological processes include:

- *Wechsler Intelligence Scales for Children,* 5th edn (Wechsler, 2014);
- *Woodcock Johnson Tests of Cognitive Abilities,* 4th edn (Schrank et al., 2014b);
- *Differential Ability Scales,* 2nd edn (Elliot, 2007);
- *Stanford–Binet Intelligence Test,* 5th edn (Roid, 2003);
- *Kaufman Assessment Battery for Children,* 2nd edn normative update (Kaufman & Kaufman, 2004).

More specific assessments of psychological processing include:

- *Behavior Rating Inventory of Executive Functions,* 2nd edn (Gioia et al., 2015);
- *Berry–Buktenica Test of Visual Motor Integration,* 6th edn (Beery, Buktenica, & Beery, 2010);

- *California Verbal Learning Test*, Children's version (Delis et al., 1994);
- *Comprehensive Test of Phonological Processing*, 2nd edn (Wagner et al., 2013);
- *Feifer Assessment of Math* (Feifer, 2016a);
- *Feifer Assessment of Reading* (Feifer, 2016b);
- *Test of Auditory Processing*, 3rd edn (Martin, Brownell, & Hamaguchi, 2018).

Psychological Processing Patterns in ASD

The most common psychological processing strengths and weaknesses that contribute to the academic achievement profiles of children with ASD include weak working memory, processing speed, and executive functioning abilities (Assouline et al., 2012; Hedvall et al., 2013; St John, Dawson, & Estes, 2017; Troyb et al., 2014b; Wang et al., 2017).

Executive functioning refers to an umbrella of mental operations such as inhibition, cognitive shifting, organization, planning, and self-monitoring. A wide variety of executive functioning abilities are negatively affected in many children with ASD; however, some areas such as cognitive ability/shift can be particularly difficult for children with ASD (Lai et al., 2017; Leung et al., 2016; Troyb et al., 2014b). This is consistent with children with ASD's "stickiness" to objects and tasks as well as their preference for routine, and other repetitive and restrictive symptoms of ASD.

Working memory refers to the ability to hold information in mind while using it to complete a task. Children with ASD often demonstrate weaknesses in this area (Assouline et al., 2012; Wang et al., 2017). Working memory can be divided into verbal working memory and visual–spatial working memory. Verbal memory is the ability to rehearse and use language-based information for short periods of time, whereas visual–spatial working memory is the ability to rehearse and use a visual representation or spatial map. Children with ASD often show weaknesses in both of these aspects of working memory (Lai et al., 2017; Wang et al., 2017). Working memory is critical to nearly every academic achievement area. Weaknesses in verbal working memory can also make it difficult for children with ASD to learn and remember verbal instruction.

Processing speed refers to the ability to complete simple tasks quickly and can include skills such as rapid automatic naming. This is an additional area of weakness for many children with ASD (Assouline et al., 2012; Hedvall et al., 2013; Oliveras-Rentas et al., 2012). Children with low processing speed abilities work slowly and struggle with work completion, the completion of tests within allotted times, and note taking. They may also become overwhelmed when they receive a large amount of information quickly and cannot process it at the necessary pace.

As mentioned in Chapter 5, there are various profiles related to verbal and nonverbal abilities. Many children with ASD demonstrate relative nonverbal strengths; however, some demonstrate a relative verbal strength (Nader, Jelenic, & Soulieres, 2015). Children with relative verbal strengths tend to be children who previously would have been identified as having Asperger's disorder.

Reading

Between 35% and 80% of students with ASD experience unexpected difficulties in one or more area of literacy, given their cognitive abilities (Solari et al., 2017). However, recent studies emphasize the heterogeneity within ASD and note that there is no single reading profile that characterizes students with ASD (Keen et al., 2016; McIntyre et al., 2017). One of the most common reading profiles reflects stronger basic reading skills than reading comprehension skills (McIntyre et al., 2017; Miller et al., 2017; Ricketts et al., 2013; Wei et al., 2015). Children may read the words of passages but be unable to understand them. This is the opposite of the pattern that is often seen in children with dyslexia, where a student might struggle to read single words, but have little difficulty comprehending stories read aloud. At this time, literature on ASD and reading focuses on early literacy, basic reading skills, and reading comprehension. Little is known about children with ASD's reading fluency skills.

Early Literacy and Basic Reading

Early literacy for young children involves learning letter names, knowing letter–sound correspondence, and understanding concepts of print. In general, there appears to be no difference in the word-reading abilities of children with and without ASD when they are matched for cognitive abilities (Jacobs & Richdale, 2013; Troyb et al., 2014a). Consistent with this, young children with ASD often show similar alphabet knowledge skills to their typically developing peers (Dynia et al., 2016).

Although they may be able to name letters, young children with ASD appear to have weaker concepts of print than their typically developing peers (Dynia et al., 2014, 2016; Westerveld et al., 2017). Concepts of print involve understanding how to handle a book, knowing the directionality of print, and distinguishing between print and illustrations. Concepts of print may be more difficult for children with ASD because they are less likely be to explicitly taught these skills and their typically developing peers may be learning more easily through observational methods.

Some children with ASD show a heightened ability to name letters and read words, or hyperlexia. Children with hyperlexia sometimes show a precocious ability to name letters, but they may lack the ability to use words to functionally communicate. For example, a two year old may identify all of the alphabet letters but be unable to request a drink. In addition, an older child may be able to read sentences at a high level, but not able to comprehend printed material at a more basic level. It is estimated that between 6% and 20% of children with ASD demonstrate symptoms of hyperlexia; however, most cases, potentially more than 80%, of hyperlexia occur in children with ASD (Ostrolenk et al., 2017). Therefore, particular attention should be paid to screening hyperlexic children for ASD.

Psychological processes such as phonological awareness, processing speed, rapid automatic naming, verbal reasoning, visual–spatial orthographic processing, and working memory are important in basic reading skills (Dehn, 2014; Flanagan, Ortiz, & Alfonso, 2013). There is no current consensus on whether or not children with ASD's phonological awareness develops similarly to children without ASD (Dynia et al., 2017; Gabig, 2010). There is some indication that children with ASD may have slower rapid automatic naming abilities than typically developing children; however, children who demonstrate hyperlexia may have particularly strong rapid automatic naming abilities (Losh, Esserman, & Piven, 2010; Wei et al., 2015). Further, weaker working memory and processing speed is associated with weaker reading abilities in children with ASD (Assouline et al., 2012).

Reading Comprehension

Reading comprehension is often cited as the most significant area of academic impairment for children with ASD (Keen et al., 2016). It is estimated that 35–58% of children with ASD have difficulties with reading comprehension (Solari et al., 2017). Throughout elementary school, children with ASD often lose ground in reading comprehension (Wei et al., 2015). In adolescence, the pattern of weaker reading comprehension compared with typically developing peers continues (Troyb et al., 2014a).

Overall, reading comprehension involves multiple psychological abilities in typically developing children such as executive functioning, long-term retrieval, nonverbal reasoning, verbal reasoning, and working memory (Dehn, 2014; Flanagan et al., 2013). Several needed abilities and psychological processes involved in reading comprehension can be weak in children with ASD. Specifically, children with ASD may struggle with verbal abilities, executive functioning, working memory, and social thinking (Finnegan & Mazin, 2016; Knight & Sartini, 2015; Ricketts et al., 2013).

Children with ASD often have weak oral language abilities; this is an area known to be important in reading comprehension. Oral language abilities affect children's ability to understand the meanings of words, draw on background knowledge, and make inferences from text. Although children with ASD may have the same syntactic language skills, or skills associated with the arrangement of words into a meaningful sentence, they do not have the same semantic language, understanding of word meaning, and pragmatic language. A lack of understanding of social language also impacts reading comprehension skills (Jacobs & Richdale, 2013).

Executive functioning and particularly working memory are related to reading comprehension skills; these areas of processing are often weak for children with ASD (Craig et al., 2016; Cutting et al., 2009; Locascio et al., 2010; Wang et al., 2017). Children rely on executive functioning abilities to monitor their understanding of text and use repair strategies, such as re-reading, when they recognize that they do not understand a passage. Also, understanding how to plan and organize reading a passage is important to reading comprehension. Planning and organization skills such as previewing passages, using text headings and graphs, and anticipating passage context strengthen understanding. Furthermore, Assouline et al. (2012) found that working memory and processing speed accounted for 61% of the variance in reading achievement for children with ASD. In relation to working memory, children must simultaneously store reading passage information, process it for understanding in tasks such as answering comprehension questions, and inhibit their attention to irrelevant information.

Social behavior and social cognition contribute to reading comprehension skills in children with ASD. Children with more deficits related to social communication demonstrate weaker reading comprehension skills (Jones et al., 2009; Ricketts et al., 2013; Westerveld et al., 2017). This area is not typically assessed in the consideration of reading comprehension problems in typically developing children, but it is relevant in assessment of children with ASD. Social cognitions are needed to understand the intentions of characters and their feelings. Social understanding can influence the ability to comprehend characters' motives and predict their actions. Consistent with this, children with ASD are likely to struggle more with texts that require social understanding and an ability to determine the mental states of characters (Brown, Oram-Cardy, & Johnson, 2013). Texts that can be interpreted on their own, without reference and integration with personal experiences in the world, are easier for children with ASD to understand. Therefore, they may struggle more with fiction texts than informational, nonfiction texts. This is consistent with the understanding that children with ASD demonstrate more expertise related to objects and information than to people and the social environment. You may find a child with ASD who devours books about historical trains, but who resists reading fictional books such as *The Boxcar Children*.

Table 6.2 Psychological processes involved in reading

	Basic reading	Reading comprehension
Psychological processes	Phonological processing Rapid automatic naming* Verbal reasoning Visual–spatial–orthographic processing Working memory*	Executive functioning* Long-term retrieval Nonverbal reasoning Verbal reasoning Working memory*

Psychological processes compiled from Dehn (2014) and Flanagan et al. (2013).

*Research indicates that these are possible areas of weakness for children with ASD.

Overall, when assessing reading skills, executive functioning, long-term retrieval, nonverbal reasoning, phonological processing, rapid automatic naming, verbal reasoning, visual–spatial–orthographic processing, and working memory should be assessed. Executive function, rapid automatic naming, and working memory are the most likely areas to be of concern for children with ASD. In addition, assessing children's social understanding is important to reading comprehension in particular.

Math

Within the domain of math, there is again a high level of heterogeneity in profiles of children with ASD (Keen et al., 2016). In fact, there are increased numbers of children with ASD who either show unexpectedly high or low math achievement given their cognitive abilities when compared with typically developing peers (Wei et al., 2015).

Some of the stereotypical views of strong math and science abilities in individuals with ASD are confirmed by high-performing students with ASD. There are some indications that children with ASD and strong math abilities may have family members in math, science, or engineering. They are more likely to become interested in careers in math, physics, and computer science themselves (Baron-Cohen et al., 2001). Furthermore, a higher percentage of college students with ASD study science, technology, engineering and mathematics (STEM) fields than exist in the general population (Wei et al., 2013).

However, a pattern of weak math skills is also seen in a subgroup of children with ASD. In spite of the stereotype that children with ASD show mathematical giftedness, it is more likely that they will demonstrate math weakness (Oswald et al., 2016; St John et al., 2017). In the group of low performing math students, similar to patterns noted within reading skills, there are indications that children with ASD have more difficulty with applied, math reasoning skills than in basic math calculation skills (Miller et al., 2017).

For typically developing children, a number of psychological processes are involved in math. Math requires abilities related to executive functioning, long-term retrieval, nonverbal reasoning, processing speed, verbal reasoning, visual–spatial reasoning, and working memory (Dehn, 2014; Flanagan et al., 2013).

Early Numeracy and Math Calculation

Some children with ASD experience greater difficulty with calculation skills than typically developing peers with similar cognitive abilities. It is estimated that about 6–40% of children with ASD have particular difficulty with math (Aagten-Murphy et al., 2015; Estes et al., 2011).

Although many children with ASD have problems with calculation, some children demonstrate hypercalculia, or unexpectedly strong math calculation skills, given their cognitive abilities. Rates of hypercalculia may range between 16% and 20% for children with average cognitive abilities (Jones et al., 2009; Wei et al., 2015).

Early numeracy skills include the ability to: (1) subitize (e.g., quickly name the number of dots seen without counting them), (2) count, (3) compare the magnitude of two groups of dots, and (4) estimate the placement of a number on a number line. There is currently no clear pattern of strengths and weaknesses in these areas for children with ASD. Some studies have found similar early numeracy skills for children with ASD versus typically developing children (Titeca et al., 2014; Turi et al., 2015); others have found weaker comparison and estimation skills in children with ASD (Aagten-Murphy et al., 2015; Hiniker, Rosenberg-Lee, & Menon, 2016). However, early numeracy skills may be differentially important for children with ASD in predicting their early math skills. For example, the ability to subitize and name a number may be particularly important for development of math skills in children with ASD, indicating that this should be a targeted area of instruction and intervention (Hiniker et al., 2016; Titeca et al., 2014).

Executive functioning and working memory abilities are important in math calculations. Children with ASD can struggle with these processing abilities and, therefore, demonstrate math calculation weaknesses. Children with ASD may have more difficulty with metacognitive monitoring of their work and in completing math algorithms. They are more likely to have difficulty assessing how likely their math calculations are correct than their peers and also tend to report that they made the errors on purpose when asked (Brosnan et al., 2016). Furthermore, executive functioning related to shifting skills is often an area of weakness for children with ASD, who may have difficulty using cognitive flexibility to shift between math calculation problems and strategies (St John et al., 2017). Therefore, you may see them make errors by continuing to use addition when subtraction is needed on subsequent items on a math assignment.

Table 6.3 Psychological processes involved in math

	Math calculation	Math problem-solving
Psychological processes	Long-term retrieval Nonverbal reasoning Processing speed* Visual–spatial processing Working memory*	Executive functioning* Long-term retrieval Nonverbal reasoning Processing speed* Verbal reasoning* Working memory*

Psychological processes compiled from Dehn (2014) and Flanagan et al. (2013).

*Research indicates that these are possible areas of weakness for children with ASD.

Math Problem-solving

Some children with ASD have weaker math reasoning skills than their peers, while others show math reasoning skills that are comparable to their peers without ASD (Bae, Chiang, & Hickson, 2015; Troyb et al., 2014a). Sometimes children with ASD who show unexpectedly strong math calculation do not show these same, exceptional strengths when it comes to math problem-solving (Iuculano et al., 2014).

For children with ASD who have more difficulty with math reasoning, their everyday math knowledge is weaker than typically developing peers (Bae et al., 2015). Everyday math knowledge can be associated with using money and understanding concepts of time. Similar to the weaknesses some children with ASD exhibit in reading comprehension, deficits related to contextual, social situations may make applied math problems more difficult. Therefore, adaptive skills related to money and time may be weak. These math-reasoning skills are particularly important for independent living in the future. Furthermore, weaknesses in executive functioning, working memory, and visual–spatial abilities negatively affect math achievement (Assouline et al., 2012).

Overall, when assessing math skills, executive functioning, long-term retrieval, nonverbal reasoning, processing speed, verbal reasoning, visual–spatial processing, and working memory should be assessed (Table 6.3). Executive function, processing speed, verbal reasoning, and working memory are the most likely areas to be of concern for children with ASD.

Written Expression

A number of studies have found that written expression can be difficult for children with ASD (Finnegan & Accardo, 2017; Mayes & Calhoun, 2008). Similar to patterns in reading and math, the rote aspects of writing may be easier than the more complex aspects for children with ASD, who may struggle more with the use of prose and story construction than in using writing conventions such as the use of punctuation or mechanics (Finnegan & Accardo, 2017; Keen et al., 2016; Troyb et al., 2014a). Children with ASD also tend to write less lengthy compositions, have poorer legibility, and write slower (Finnegan & Accardo, 2017; Zajic et al., 2016). Although individuals with ASD show weaknesses in written expression across genres (e.g., narrative, expository, and persuasive) compared with typical peers, some genres of writing are more difficult for individuals with ASD (Brown & Klein, 2011). In particular, there is evidence that persuasive writing is more difficult due to the need to take on the reader's perspective (Brown et al., 2014).

Written expression is one the most complex academic skills. Writing an essay involves integrating many psychological processes, including executive functioning, long-term retrieval, nonverbal reasoning, phonological processing, processing speed, verbal reasoning, orthographic processing, and working memory (Dehn, 2014; Flanagan et al., 2013). Weaknesses in psychological processes such as working memory, executive functioning, processing speed, and theory of mind are associated with weaknesses in written expression for children with ASD (Assouline et al., 2012; Brown & Klein, 2011; St John et al., 2017). Related to working memory, students must simultaneously consider mechanical aspects of writing, the content of their piece, and the overall organization or theme of their writing. Executive functioning encompasses aspects of writing such as planning and organizing the piece as well as monitoring their progress. Students can also have difficulty shifting their ideas to fit the required writing prompt. Slow processing speed abilities can cause writing tasks to become slow and laborious, often contributing to a dislike of writing tasks.

As in reading comprehension, social understanding and theory of mind are especially relevant to children with ASD's writing abilities. Students must learn to include details that allow a reader to follow their writing. Lower theory of mind abilities are associated with lower-quality, written expression pieces (Brown & Klein, 2011). Weaknesses in theory of mind likely affect a student's ability to incorporate aspects of social understanding and perspective taking.

Overall, when assessing writing skills, executive functioning, long-term retrieval, phonological processing, processing speed, verbal reasoning, visual–spatial–orthographic processing, and working memory should be assessed (Table 6.4). Executive function, processing speed, and working memory are the most likely areas to be of concern for children with ASD. Consideration of how a child with ASD's social communication weakness may translate into weaknesses in written expression should also be considered.

Table 6.4 Psychological processes involved in written expression

	Written expression
Psychological processes	Executive functioning*
	Long-term retrieval
	Nonverbal reasoning
	Phonological processing (spelling)
	Processing speed*
	Verbal reasoning
	Visual–spatial–orthographic processing
	Working memory*

Psychological processes compiled from Dehn (2014) and Flanagan et al. (2013).

*Research indicates that these are possible areas of weakness for children with ASD.

Case Study 1

Harun is an 8-year, 7-month-old boy who is eligible for special education in the areas of significant developmental delay and speech–language impairment. He was referred for an evaluation to determine a possible area of categorical eligibility. The team suspects that he has an ASD. They would also like information about his weak academic skills. His mother wonders if he has a learning disability.

Harun was born full term with no birth complications. There is no known relevant medical history or diagnosis. His motor skills developed on time; however, he did not begin to speak until age 3 years. His mother's first concerns were about his delayed speech.

Harun's teacher, Ms. Ruiz, reported that one of Harun's strengths is his willingness to try academic tasks. Harun's performance in reading and math is below grade level. In reading, he struggles with retelling the main event, reading fluently, sequencing ideas, and comprehending texts. In math, multi-step word problems area a challenge. In writing, Harun struggles to organize his ideas and transfer information from a graphic organizer into a paragraph. Socially, he gets frustrated that he does not have friends. He will occasionally shut down and lose focus on tasks. He tends to talk at people rather than with them. Harun is obsessed with videogames, more than other boys his age. Assessment results include the following:

(continued)

(continued)

> Differential Ability Scales, 2nd edn (DAS-II): Verbal: 83; Nonverbal: 111; Spatial: 102; GCA: 99; SNC: 108.
>
> Woodcock–Johnson IV – Tests of Cognitive Ability: Processing Speed: 61; Short-term Memory: 84; Long-term Retrieval: 96.
>
> Beery–Buktenica Developmental Test of Visual–Motor Integration, 6th edn (VMI): SS: 85.
>
> NEPSY-II: Affect Recognition: 1; Theory of Mind: 4.
>
> Woodcock–Johnson IV – Tests of Achievement: Letter–Word Identification: 98; Passage Comprehension: 89; Reading Fluency: 90; Calculation: 118; Applied Problems: 88; Math Fluency: 81; Writing Samples 89; Spelling: 101.
>
> Test of Pragmatic Language: SS = 64.
>
> Oral and Written Language Scales: Listening Comprehension: 80; Oral Expression: 72; Composite: 74.
>
> Comprehensive Assessment of Spoken Language: Antonyms: 89; Syntax Construction: 62; Paragraph Comprehension: 59; Non-literal Language: 72; Core Composite: 68.
>
> Adaptive Behavior Assessment System, 2nd edn (ABAS-3), Parent: Conceptual: 72; Social: 61; Practical: 83; General Adaptive Composite: 68.
>
> Adaptive Behavior Assessment System, 2nd edn (ABAS-3), Teacher: Conceptual: 80; Social: 65; Practical: 77; General Adaptive Composite: 73.
>
> Childhood Autism Rating Scale, 2nd edition, High Functioning: Score in the Mild-to-Moderate range.
>
> What academic strengths and weaknesses can you identify? How does this pattern fit with a student who may have an ASD?
>
> What psychological processing strengths and weaknesses can you identify? How does this pattern fit with a student who may have an ASD?
>
> What area(s) of eligibility would you consider?

References

Aagten-Murphy, D., Attucci, C., Daniel, N., Klaric, E., Burr, D., & Pellicano, E. (2015). Numerical estimation in children with autism. *Autism Research*, 8(6), 668–681. doi:10.1002/aur.1482.

Assouline, S., Foley Nicpon, M., & Dockery, L. (2012). Predicting the academic achievement of gifted students with autism spectrum disorder. *Journal of*

Autism & Developmental Disorders, 42(9), 1781–1789. doi:10.1007/s10803-011-1403-x.

Bae, Y., Chiang, H.-M., & Hickson, L. (2015). Mathematical word problem solving ability of children with autism spectrum disorder and their typically developing peers. *Journal of Autism & Developmental Disorders*, 45(7), 2200–2208. doi:10.1007/s10803-015-2387-8.

Baron-Cohen, S., Wheelwright, S., Skinner, R., Martin, J., & Clubley, E. (2001). The autism-spectrum quotient (AQ): Evidence from Asperger syndrome/high-functioning autism, males and females, scientists and mathematicians. *Journal of Autism & Developmental Disorders*, 31(1), 5–17.

Beery, K. E., Buktenica, N. A., & Beery, N. A. (2010). *Berry–Butenica Test of Visual Motor Integration – 6*. Minneapolis, MN: Pearson.

Brosnan, M., Johnson, H., Grawemeyer, B., Chapman, E., Antoniadou, K., & Hollinworth, M. (2016). Deficits in metacognitive monitoring in mathematics assessments in learners with autism spectrum disorder. *Autism*, 20(4), 463–472. doi:10.1177/1362361315589477,

Brown, H. & Klein, P. (2011). Writing, Asperger syndrome and theory of mind. *Journal of Autism & Developmental Disorders*, 41(11), 1464–1474. doi:10.1007/s10803-010-1168-7.

Brown, H., Oram-Cardy, J., & Johnson, A. (2013). A meta-analysis of the reading comprehension skills of individuals on the autism spectrum. *Journal of Autism & Developmental Disorders*, 43(4), 932–955. doi:10.1007/s10803-012-1638-1.

Brown, H. M., Johnson, A. M., Smyth, R. E., & Oram Cardy, J. (2014). Exploring the persuasive writing skills of students with high-functioning autism spectrum disorder. *Research in Autism Spectrum Disorders*, 8(11), 1482–1499. doi:https://doi.org/10.1016/j.rasd.2014.07.017.

Craig, F., Margari, F., Legrottaglie, A. R., Palumbi, R., de Giambattista, C., & Margari, L. (2016). A review of executive function deficits in autism spectrum disorder and attention-deficit/hyperactivity disorder. *Neuropsychiatric Disorders and Treatment*, 12, 1191–1202. doi:10.2147/ndt.s104620.

Cutting, L. E., Materek, A., Cole, C. A., Levine, T. M., & Mahone, E. M. (2009). Effects of fluency, oral language, and executive function on reading comprehension performance. *Annuals of Dyslexia*, 59(1), 34–54. doi:10.1007/s11881-009-0022-0.

Dehn, M. J. (2014). *Essentials of Processing Assessment*, 2nd edn. Hoboken, NJ: John Wiley & Sons, Inc.

Delis, D., Kramer, J. H., Kaplan, E., & Ober, B. A. (1994). *California Verbal Learning Test* – Children's version. San Antonio, TX: The Psychological Corporation.

Dynia, J. M., Lawton, K., Logan, J. A. R., & Justice, L. M. (2014). Comparing emergent-literacy skills and home-literacy environment of children with Autism and their peers. *Topics In Early Childhood Special Education*, 34(3), 142–153. doi:10.1177/0271121414536784.

Dynia, J., Brock, M., Logan, J., Justice, L., & Kaderavek, J. (2016). Comparing children with ASD and their peers' growth in print knowledge. *Journal of Autism & Developmental Disorders*, 46(7), 2490–2500. doi:10.1007/s10803-016-2790-9.

Dynia, J. M., Brock, M. E., Justice, L. M., & Kaderavek, J. N. (2017). Predictors of decoding for children with autism spectrum disorder in comparison to their peers. *Research in Autism Spectrum Disorders*, 37(Suppl C), 41–48. doi:org/10.1016/j.rasd.2017.02.003.

Elliot, C. D. (2007). *Differential Ability Scales*, 2nd edn. San Antonio, TX: Harcourt.

Estes, A., Rivera, V., Bryan, M., Cali, P., & Dawson, G. (2011). Discrepancies between academic achievement and intellectual ability in higher-functioning school-aged children with autism spectrum disorder. *Journal of Autism & Developmental Disorders*, 41(8), 1044–1052. doi:10.1007/s10803-010-1127-3.

Feifer, S. G. (2016a). *Feifer Assessment of Math*. Sparta, WI: Schoolhouse Educational Services.

Feifer, S. G. (2016b). *Feifer Assessment of Reading*. Sparta, WI: Schoolhouse Educational Services.

Finnegan, E. & Accardo, A. L. (2017). Written expression in individuals with autism spectrum disorder: A meta-analysis. *Journal of Autism & Developmental Disorders*, 48(3), 868–882. doi:10.1007/s10803-017-3385-9.

Finnegan, E. & Mazin, A. L. (2016). Strategies for increasing reading comprehension skills in students with autism spectrum disorder: A review of the literature. *Education & Treatment of Children*, 39(2), 187–219.

Flanagan, D. P., Ortiz, S. O., & Alfonso, V. C. (2013). *Essentials of Cross-battery Assessment*, 3rd edn. Hoboken, NJ: John Wiley & Sons, Inc.

Gabig, C. S. (2010). Phonological awareness and word recognition in reading by children with autism. *Communication Disorders Quarterly*, 31(2), 67–85. doi:10.1177/1525740108328410.

Gioia, G., Isquith, P. K., Guy, S. C., & Kenworthy, L. (2015). *Behavior Rating Inventory of Executive Function – 2*. Odessa, FL: Psychological Assessment Resources.

Hedvall, A., Fernell, E., Holm, A., Asberg Johnels, J., Gillberg, C., & Billstedt, E. (2013). Autism, processing speed, and adaptive functioning in preschool children. *Scientific World Journal*, Art. ID 158263. doi:10.1155/2013/158263.

Hiniker, A., Rosenberg-Lee, M., & Menon, V. (2016). Distinctive role of symbolic number sense in mediating the mathematical abilities of children with autism. *Journal of Autism & Developmental Disorders*, 46(4), 1268–1281. doi:10.1007/s10803-015-2666-4.

Iuculano, T., Rosenberg-Lee, M., Supekar, K., Lynch, C.J., Khouzam, A., Phillips, J., et al. (2014). Brain organization underlying superior mathematical abilities in children with autism. *Biological Psychiatry*, 75(3), 223–230. doi:https://doi.org/10.1016/j.biopsych.2013.06.018.

Jacobs, D. W. & Richdale, A. L. (2013). Predicting literacy in children with a high-functioning autism spectrum disorder. *Research in Developmental Disabilities*, 34(8), 2379–2390. doi:10.1016/j.ridd.2013.04.007.

Jones, C. R., Happe, F., Golden, H., Marsden, A. J., Tregay, J., Simonoff, E., et al (2009). Reading and arithmetic in adolescents with autism spectrum disorders: peaks and dips in attainment. *Neuropsychology*, 23(6), 718–728. doi:10.1037/a0016360.

Kaufman, A. S. & Kaufman, N. L. (2004). *Kaufman Assessment Battery for Children*, 2nd edn. Bloomington, MN: Pearson.

Kaufman, A. S. & Kaufman, N. L. (2014). *Kaufman Test of Educational Achievement – 3*. Bloomington, MN: NCS Pearson.

Keen, D., Webster, A., & Ridley, G. (2016). How well are children with autism spectrum disorder doing academically at school? An overview of the literature. *Autism: International Journal of Research & Practice*, 20(3), 276–294. doi:10.1177/136236131558096

Kim, S. H., Bal, V. H., & Lord, C. (2017). Longitudinal follow-up of academic achievement in children with autism from age 2 to 18. *Journal of Child Psychology and Psychiatry*, 59(3), 258–267. doi:10.1111/jcpp.12808.

Knight, V. & Sartini, E. (2015). A comprehensive literature review of comprehension strategies in core content areas for students with autism spectrum disorder. *Journal of Autism & Developmental Disorders*, 45(5), 1213–1229. doi:10.1007/s10803-014-2280-x.

Lai, C. L. E., Lau, Z., Lui, S. S. Y., Lok, E., Tam, V., Chan, Q., et al. (2017). Meta-analysis of neuropsychological measures of executive functioning in children and adolescents with high-functioning autism spectrum disorder. *Autism Research*, 10(5), 911–939. doi:10.1002/aur.1723.

Leung, R. C., Vogan, V. M., Powell, T. L., Anagnostou, E., & Taylor, M. J. (2016). The role of executive functions in social impairment in autism spectrum disorder. *Child Neuropsychology*, 22(3), 336–344. doi:10.1080/09297049.2015.1005066.

Locascio, G., Mahone, E. M., Eason, S. H., & Cutting, L. E. (2010). Executive dysfunction among children with reading comprehension deficits. *Journal of Learning Disabilities*, 43(5), 441–454. doi:10.1177/0022219409355476.

Losh, M., Esserman, D., & Piven, J. (2010). Rapid automatized naming as an index of genetic liability to autism. *Journal of Neurodevelopmental Disorder*, 2(2), 109–116. doi:10.1007/s11689-010-9045-4.

McIntyre, N. S., Solari, E. J., Grimm, R. P., Lerro, L. E., Gonzales, J. E., & Mundy, P. C. (2017). A comprehensive examination of reading heterogeneity in students with high functioning autism: Distinct reading profiles and their relation to autism symptom severity. *Journal of Autism and Developmental Disorders*, 47(4), 1086-1101. doi:10.1007/s10803-017-3029-

Martin, N., Brownell, R., & Hamaguchi, P. (2018). *Test of Auditory Processing – 4*. Torrance, CA: Western Psychological Services.

Mayes, S. D. & Calhoun, S. L. (2008). WISC-IV and WIAT-II profiles in children with high-functioning autism. *Journal of Autism & Developmental Disorders*, 38(3), 428–439. doi:10.1007/s10803-007-0410-4.

Miller, L. E., Burke, J. D., Troyb, E., Knoch, K., Herlihy, L. E., & Fein, D. A. (2017). Preschool predictors of school-age academic achievement in autism spectrum disorder. *Clinical Neuropsychologist*, 31(2), 382–403. doi:10.1080/13854046.2016.1225665.

Nader, A. M., Jelenic, P., & Soulieres, I. (2015). Discrepancy between WISC-III and WISC-IV cognitive profile in autism spectrum: What does it reveal about autistic cognition? *PLoS One*, 10(12), e0144645. doi:10.1371/journal.pone.0144645.

Oliveras-Rentas, R. E., Kenworthy, L., Roberson, R. B., 3rd, Martin, A., & Wallace, G. L. (2012). WISC-IV profile in high-functioning autism spectrum disorders: impaired processing speed is associated with increased autism communication symptoms and decreased adaptive communication abilities. *Journal of Autism and Developmental Disorders*, 42(5), 655–664. doi:10.1007/s10803-011-1289-7.

Ostrolenk, A., Forgeot d'Arc, B., Jelenic, P., Samson, F., & Mottron, L. (2017). Hyperlexia: Systematic review, neurocognitive modelling, and outcome. *Neuroscience & Biobehavioral Reviews*, 79, 134–149. doi:10.1016/j.neubiorev.2017.04.029.

Oswald, T. M., Beck, J. S., Iosif, A. M., McCauley, J. B., Gilhooly, L. J., Matter, J. C., & Solomon, M. (2016). Clinical and cognitive characteristics associated with mathematics problem solving in adolescents with autism spectrum disorder. *Autism Research*, 9(4), 480–490. doi:10.1002/aur.1524.

Ricketts, J., Jones, C., Happé, F., & Charman, T. (2013). Reading comprehension in autism spectrum disorders: The role of oral language and social functioning. *Journal of Autism & Developmental Disorders*, 43(4), 807–816. doi:10.1007/s10803-012-1619-4.

Roid, G. H. (2003). *Stanford–Binet Intelligence Scales*, 5th edn. Torrance, CA: Western Psychological Services.

St John, T., Dawson, G., & Estes, A. (2017). Brief report: Executive function as a predictor of academic achievement in school-aged children with ASD. *Journal of Autism & Developmental Disorders*, 48(1): 276–283. doi:10.1007/s10803-017-3296-9.

Schrank, F. A., McGrew, K. S., Mather, N., & Woodcock, R. W. (2014a). *Woodcock–Johnson IV Tests of Achievement*. Rolling Meadows: IL: Riverside Publishing. Los Angeles, CA: Western Psychological Services.

Schrank, F. A., McGrew, K. S., Mather, N., & Woodcock, R. W. (2014b). *Woodcock–Johnson IV Tests of Cognitive Abilities*. Rolling Meadows, IL: Riverside Publishing.

Solari, E., Grimm, R., McIntyre, N., Swain-Lerro, L., Zajic, M., & Mundy, P. (2017). The relation between text reading fluency and reading comprehension for students with autism spectrum disorders. *Research in Autism Spectrum Disorders*, 41–42, 8–19.

Titeca, D., Roeyers, H., Josephy, H., Ceulemans, A., & Desoete, A. (2014). Preschool predictors of mathematics in first grade children with autism spectrum disorder. *Research in Developmental Disabilities*, 35(11), 2714–2727. doi:10.1016/j.ridd.2014.07.012.

Troyb, E., Orinstein, A., Tyson, K., Helt, M., Eigsti, I. M., Stevens, M., & Fein, D. (2014a). Academic abilities in children and adolescents with a history of autism spectrum disorders who have achieved optimal outcomes. *Autism*, 18(3), 233–243. doi:10.1177/1362361312473519.

Troyb, E., Rosenthal, M., Eigsti, I. M., Kelley, E., Tyson, K., Orinstein, A., et al. (2014b). Executive functioning in individuals with a history of ASDs who have achieved optimal outcomes. *Child Neuropsychology* 20(4), 378–397. doi:10.1080/09297049.2013.799644.

Turi, M., Burr, D. C., Igliozzi, R., Aagten-Murphy, D., Muratori, F., & Pellicano, E. (2015). Children with autism spectrum disorder show reduced adaptation to number. *Proceedings of the National Academy of Sciences of the United States of America*, 112(25), 7868–7872. doi:10.1073/pnas.1504099112.

Wagner, R., Torgesen, J., Rashotte, C., & Pearson, N. A. (2013). *Comprehensive Test of Phonological Processing*, 2nd edn. Austin, TX: PRO-Ed.

Wang, Y., Zhang, Y. B., Liu, L. L., Cui, J. F., Wang, J., Shum, D. H., et al. (2017). A meta-analysis of working memory impairments in autism spectrum disorders. *Neuropsychology Review*, 27(1), 46–61. doi:10.1007/s11065-016-9336-y.

Wechsler, D. (2009). *Wechsler Individual Achievement Test – 3*. Bloomington, MN: Pearson.

Wechsler, D. (2014). *Wechsler Intelligence Scale for Children*, 5th edn. Bloomington, MN: Pearson.

Wei, X., Yu, J. W., Shattuck, P., McCracken, M., & Blackorby, J. (2013). Science, technology, engineering, and mathematics (STEM) participation among college students with an autism spectrum disorder. *Journal of Autism and Developmental Disorders*, 43(7), 1539–1546. doi:10.1007/s10803-012-1700-z.

Wei, X., Christiano, E. R. A., Yu, J. W., Wagner, M., & Spiker, D. (2015). Reading and math achievement profiles and longitudinal growth trajectories of children with an autism spectrum disorder. *Autism: The International Journal of Research & Practice*, 19(2), 200–210. doi:10.1177/1362361313516549.

Westerveld, M., Paynter, J., Trembath, D., Webster, A., Hodge, A., & Roberts, J. (2017). The emergent literacy skills of preschool children with autism spectrum disorder. *Journal of Autism & Developmental Disorders*, 47(2), 424–438. doi:10.1007/s10803-016-2964-5.

Zajic, M.C., McIntyre, N., Swain-Lerro, L., Novotny, S., Oswald, T., & Mundy, P. (2016). Attention and written expression in school-age, high-functioning children with autism spectrum disorders. *Autism*, 22(3): 245–258. doi:10.1177/1362361316675121.

Part III

ASD Identification in Schools

Chapter 7

The Process of Identification of ASD in Schools

Schools provide significant support for children with autism spectrum disorders (ASD). Although the medical system relies on the Diagnostic and Statistical Manual of Mental Disorders, 5th edn (DSM-V) to diagnose ASD, two federal laws regulate the services for children with ASD within schools, namely the Individuals with Disabilities Education Act (IDEA) and Section 504 of the Rehabilitation Act. Under the IDEA, children with disabilities are entitled to special education services that provide a Free and Appropriate Education (FAPE) in the Least Restrictive Environment (LRE). The Office of Special Education administers IDEA for children aged 3–21. Section 504 of the Rehabilitation Act also protects the rights

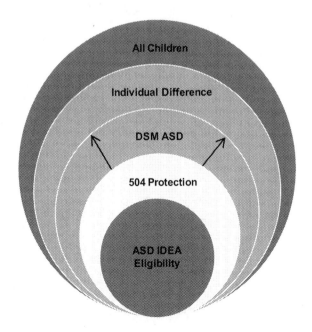

Figure 7.1 ASD and related public school services

of children with disabilities, ensuring that they do not experience discrimination. Within the Department of Education, the Office of Civil Rights administrates Section 504, which is a broad law that covers the lifespan and safeguards the rights of people with disabilities in many areas of their lives, including employment, public access to buildings, transportation, and education. As Section 504 is broader than IDEA, it includes individuals who may not qualify for special education services under IDEA. However, all students who receive special education services are likely protected by Section 504 (Figure 7.1).

> **Tips for Talking with Families I**
>
> Some children, while demonstrating some individual differences from their peers, may not have an ASD. These differences may be apparent, but they may not negatively impact a child's function and, therefore, they may not qualify for special education or a 504 Plan. This can be difficult for families or school professionals to understand. Although these children may not qualify for additional services, their individual differences may cause them to be more susceptible to environmental influence. Therefore, the adults may need to pay more attention to the child–environment fit. The following illustration from Boyce and Ellis (2005) may be helpful in explaining this.
>
> If you imagine children are flowers, many children are dandelions. They can thrive almost anywhere through any condition of drought, rain, soil, and sun. In contrast, there are a few beautiful orchids. However, orchids are much more reactive to their environment. They require close attention and nurturing. With this nurturance, they can grow to have particular beauty. Your child is more an orchid. His fit with his environment is particularly important to his growth. We may need to look more closely at whom we select as his teacher, which courses are placed on his schedule, and which extracurricular activities are selected. (Adapted from Boyce and Ellis, 2005.)

Age 0–3 Years ASD Identification: IDEA Part C Eligibility

Children aged 0–3 years who are identified as having a developmental delay are eligible for early intervention services through IDEA Part C, Infants and Toddlers with Disabilities. All 50 states and the District of Columbia currently participate in the voluntary Part C of IDEA; however, the implementation of the program varies considerably across the 50 states (Stahmer & Mandell, 2007). Services are typically provided through state public health departments, but they are sometimes administered through state educational departments. The state public health departments coordinate Part C services in about two-thirds of states (Stahmer & Mandell, 2007). Qualification criteria for IDEA Part C services are more general than for IDEA Part B services which are provided for school-age children. Forty-four states and the District of Columbia specifically identify autism spectrum disorders as an area of eligibility for Part C, whereas seven states do not specifically recognize ASD as an eligible disability (Barton et al., 2016). Although children may qualify due to a specific diagnosis, such as ASD, many children qualify without a specific diagnosis but due to general developmental delays as defined by the individual states. An Individualized Family Service Plan is created for children qualifying for IDEA Part C. Services are often provided in a child's home.

School-based ASD Identification: IDEA Part B Eligibility

In 1990, autism was first identified as an area of eligibility for special education (Barton et al., 2016). ASD is one of thirteen areas of eligibility identified under IDEA. The current federal definition of autism states:

> *Autism* means a developmental disability significantly affecting verbal and nonverbal communication and social interaction, generally evident before age three, that adversely affects a child's educational performance. Other characteristics often associated with autism are engagement in repetitive activities and stereotyped movements, resistance to environmental change or change in daily routines, and unusual responses to sensory experiences.
>
> 34 CFR 300.8 (c) (1) (i)

The federal definition also states that "Autism does not apply if a child's educational performance is adversely affected primarily because the child has an emotional disturbance" and allows for identification after age 3.

Although federal guidelines set the general eligibility criteria for ASD, each state must interpret these guidelines to establish state criteria that meet or exceed the federal guidelines. Therefore, there are some variations in the definition across the 50 states and the District of Columbia. Barton et al. (2016) found that 41 states use the exact federal definition, whereas 10 states alter the definition.

Much of the federal definition for autism is fairly consistent with the DSM-V ASD criteria; however, the IDEA definition also emphasizes that a child's educational performance must be adversely affected. A common misperception is that educational performance refers to academic performance; however, educational performance in fact includes a child's performance in academic, functional, social, and behavioral domains within school. For some children with ASD, they may not have problems keeping up with the academic requirements of school, but they may struggle with the social and behavioral expectations of school and, therefore, require specialized instruction.

A 2007 letter from the Office of Special Education and Rehabilitation Services provided clarification regarding the meaning of educational performance. Alexa Posney, the then Director of the Office of Special Education Programs, wrote:

> It remains the Department's position that the term "educational performance" as used in the IDEA and its implementing regulations is not limited to academic performance . . . IDEA and the regulations clearly establish that the determination about whether a child is a child with a disability is not limited to information about the child's academic performance.
>
> (Posney, 2007)

In 2015, the Sixth Circuit of Appeals provided further clarification regarding educational performance in the case of *Q.W. v. Board of Education of Fayette County* 2015. The case involved a child who was no longer eligible for a special education individualized educational plan or program (IEP) because his autism no longer adversely affected his educational performance. The court affirmed that educational performance may include academic, social, and behavioral domains; however, the court's decision noted that adverse impact on education performance must be shown in the classroom or school experience. Social and behavioral deficits that occurred only at home were not sufficient to entitle a student to special education services.

Related to the assessments that can be used to establish eligibility in the area of autism, requirements vary across states. Barton et al. (2016) found that at least 25 states allow non-district evaluations to determine eligibility in the area of ASD. Commonly accepted reports came from professionals such as psychiatrists and psychologists. The study found that relatively few states will accept reports from speech and language therapists to establish an ASD eligibility. Six states' regulations allow non-district diagnoses or evaluations from qualified individuals with specialized training in ASD. Although local traditional or state regulations may require a medical diagnosis of ASD, federal ASD eligibility criteria do not require a medical diagnosis. In fact, many times school psychologists will be more equipped to conduct an appropriate evaluation for suspected ASD than a child's pediatrician. The vast majority of states do not require a physician or medical diagnosis of ASD.

Early Transition Services

Before age 3 years, the transition to IDEA Part B (i.e., school-age services) from IDEA Part C (i.e., 0–3 years services) begins. At this point, children transition from family-centered services to educationally focused services. If a child qualifies for IDEA Part B services, the first IEP is written.

Preschool Services

In addition to children who are transitioning from IDEA Part C services, some children may be initially referred by their family or other professionals for an evaluation to determine possible special education eligibility during their preschool years. Community preschools may be the first to express concerns to parents about a child's functioning. It is important that an evaluation for an ASD be conducted when concerns arise related to children's communication, social interactions, and behavioral differences. Some children with ASD may not qualify for services if an evaluation assesses only for possible eligibility in the area of significant developmental delay (SDD). This is more likely to happen for children with average cognitive, receptive, and expressive language abilities. More sensitive measures, related to children's social communication and interaction, as well as emotional/behavioral regulation, are needed in order to identify areas of weakness and potential educational impact for these children.

Although research indicates that ASD can be reliably diagnosed by age 2 years, some children are not identified until some point in elementary school (Lord et al., 2006). A common practice within public schools is to assess and identify young children as being eligible in the area of SSD rather than ASD. Later, when children grow out of the age eligibility in the area of SSD, a reevaluation may be more thorough, assessing for ASD.

School professionals may have a number of reasons for not establishing an ASD eligibility for young children, which may include beliefs that a child will receive whichever services he or she needs regardless of the area of eligibility, families need time to adjust to the idea that the child has some delays before an ASD is identified, and children need access to structured, school settings before ASD can be identified. Sometimes school psychologists do not feel they have the appropriate training to assess preschoolers. In addition, local policies, a lack of school psychologists to conduct the evaluation, and a lack of funding to conduct more comprehensive ASD assessments may also contribute to this practice. These beliefs and policies are likely harmful to children with ASD. A failure to identify an ASD when possible may cause children to miss the opportunity to engage in ASD-specific intervention. This may occur within schools due to *de facto* policies that require an ASD eligibility to access an ASD-specific classroom as well as related to private insurance ASD benefits. There is no evidence that parents respond better to finding out their child has ASD when they are older or that exposure to a school setting changes the presentation of core ASD symptoms. Related to local policies and a lack of resources, school psychologists need to advocate for policies that support the early identification of ASD and the related benefits of early intervention for the child, as well as possible long-term financial benefits for the school district. New policies and resources are needed as the science of autism progresses.

Case Study 1

Elizabeth is a 3-year-old girl. Her speech milestones occurred on time. She demonstrates echolalia, repeating what others say, especially when anxious. She asks the same question repetitively. For example, "Is the printer black?" When around other children, Elizabeth will sometimes keep to herself.

Elizabeth becomes upset when there are changes in routines and separating from her mother. She will become very repetitive. Elizabeth sometimes walks in circles and likes to jump on her trampoline. She frequently plays with her LOL dolls, engaging in some basic pretend play. Elizabeth watches YouTube Kids, specifically LOL dolls.

Elizabeth has separation anxiety. She will talk about missing her brother. Elizabeth will get upset if her grandmother picks her up from school and she has not been warned.

Elizabeth has problems sleeping and takes melatonin on the advice of her pediatrician. She takes formula through a bottle several times a day to maintain weight. She will not eat food that has a scent.

Elizabeth was evaluated for special education services by the local school district. The following scores were obtained:

The Battelle Developmental Inventory, 2nd edn (BDI-2) was completed.

Adaptive: 95; Personal–Social: 92; Communication: 118; Motor: 104; Cognitive: 120.

The team concluded that Elizabeth appears to be a bright, happy, and engaging child with a supportive family network. Her skills appear to be within normal limits across all domains at this time; therefore, she does not qualify for services in the area of significant developmental delay.

- What factors may be contributing to the difficulty in identifying Elizabeth's ASD?
- What additional assessment may be necessary?

Implementation of Response to Intervention for Children Suspected of ASD

School psychologists may initially become aware of a child with possible concerns related to ASD through an RTI meeting. The general components of RTI include a universal screening, evidence-based intervention for students identified as needing intervention through the universal screening, increasing levels of intervention support, and progress monitoring for students receiving intervention. In some areas, the RTI process may be enacted by student support teams (SSTs) or multi-tiered system of supports (MTSSs).

In young children, parents and teachers may be more likely to identify a language delay or disruptive behaviors than some of the social communication problems core to ASD. Therefore, the RTI process can assist in more fully identifying a child's problems. Although little is known about the initial presenting RTI concerns for children with ASD, for children already identified as having an ASD within the schools, problems behaviors and social difficulties are often the most concerning symptom for teachers and parents (Azad & Mandell, 2016). Therefore, school psychologists should screen for a possible ASD when any child is described as experiencing behavioral and/or social problems. Although a rating scale could be used for a screening, school psychologists may informally gather similar information by asking the child's teacher and parents questions about a child's functioning and developmental history.

Table 7.1 Possible presenting RTI concerns for children with ASD

- Expressive language delay
- Weak ability to follow instructions
- Behavioral problems
- Social problems
- Poor oral recall or reading comprehension
- Anxiety
- Sensory sensitivities

Although the RTI process aims to be a collaborative process between parents and teachers, the latter tend to direct the problem identification and intervention process (Azad et al., 2016). When a possible ASD is in question, including the parents in the problem identification process can be particularly important. As ASD is a developmental disability that exists before a child enters school, parents hold critical developmental history information. Every effort should be made to include parents at the RTI stage.

RTI should target social communication and interaction or emotional/behavioral regulation for intervention. It can be a challenge to identify interventions that a teacher can implement. Possible interventions may focus on increasing a child's positive behavior during transitions from the playground using a visual timer and schedule, increasing a child's self-monitoring of work completion using a behavior chart, or increasing a child's initiation of interactions through explicit teaching and use of social stories. If a teacher or specialist is available to implement a more sustained intervention, programs such as Unstuck and On Target or PEERS are appropriate (Cannon et al., 2018; Laugeson, 2013). These programs aim to increase executive functioning and social skills in children with ASD.

Tips for Talking with Families 2

ASD Concerns in RTI

When a RTI meeting is called, parents often feel overwhelmed. There are often many people in the room and the process is unfamiliar. Use best practices in introducing the members of the team, communicating the purpose of the meeting, explaining the RTI process, and providing adequate time to hear parents' concerns. Work to provide the same opportunity for the parents to share about their child's strengths, behavior, and functioning at home as is provided for teachers to share about the child's functioning at school. Unlike some disabilities such as reading disabilities, which tend to be more apparent in an academic setting, ASD symptoms should be present across contexts. Expect parents to have critical information such as developmental history which is needed so that the team can make appropriate recommendations.

Parents, and possibly teachers, may not have considered the possible presence of an ASD. The RTI process can be a part of the gradual process of helping a parent understand their child and their child's unique characteristics. Rather than waiting to mention an ASD until you are delivering feedback results, view RTI as a process for gradually sharing concerns related to ASD and preparing parents for a possible ASD eligibility. This can make eligibility meetings go much more smoothly. In order to bring up the possibility of an ASD, you might say the following:

- Some of the difficulties you are describing remind me of problems children on the autism spectrum might show.
- Have you ever wondered if your child might show some symptoms of an ASD?
- Has anyone ever mentioned possible concerns about an ASD?

Keeping a position of curiosity and optimism about helping their child can alleviate some of the anxiety that parents may be feeling. Also, although teachers may be reporting a number of negative behaviors, help the team focus on finding appropriate interventions and avoid "admiring the problem." Acknowledge and validate the teacher's frustration concerning any negative behaviors and then move on.

Stress the problem-solving nature of the RTI process and encourage the parents to do their own research on ASD. Provide them with reliable websites to research ASD on their own. The Autism Speaks (www.autismspeaks.org) and Autism Navigator (www.autismnavigator.com) websites can be helpful.

Case Study 2

Dominick is a 5-year-old boy in kindergarten. His teacher has noted he has had behavioral problems since the beginning of the year. It is now January and you have been called to an RTI meeting. The teacher is exhausted. Dominick's strengths are described as his ability to name letters and numbers as well as rote count to 100. Dominick's teacher describes her concerns as his lack of attention to whole group instruction and behavior problems. Dominick has received two day-long suspensions for physically kicking and hitting other children. Dominick's parents report that there were some problems in preschool; however, he was always described as a "smart little boy." His family thinks he will likely become an architect when he grows up. At home, his parents have little difficulty with him. He is an only child who likes to play with puzzles for hours at time.

- What are your possible hypotheses regarding Dominick's problems?
- As the school psychologist, what questions do you have to help further define the problem?

(continued)

(continued)

Additional Information

During the course of the meeting, you gain more information about Dominick's history. His speech was delayed, but then he began speaking in full sentences around the age of 2½ years old. Dominick is described as being very focused on the fire department and as having sensitivity to clothing and sounds. Dominick has particular difficulty transitioning between activities during the day. Dominick currently has outbursts four or more times daily during transitions.

RTI Plan

As a team you decide to work to decrease Dominick's behavioral outbursts defined as crying and failing to comply with directions within 10 seconds during transitions.

Intervention: Provide Dominick with a visual schedule of his day on his desk and a laminated copy that travels with him to other areas of the building. Use a visual and bell to indicate when Dominick has three minutes before a transition. Dominick will be taught about his visual schedule daily and will receive reminder lessons on the use of the visual/bell before transitions.

Goal: Dominick will have one or fewer outbursts a day during the eight defined transitions per day.

Progress monitoring: Teacher will record number of outbursts occurring during the eight defined transitions each day.

Does the RTI Model Fit for Children with Suspected ASD?

Although federal law does not require the use of an RTI, MTSS, or SST process in order to consider special education eligibility in the area of ASD, this process may be used. The logistics, appropriateness, and effectiveness of using an RTI model for the identification of ASD eligibility is not clear (Hammond, Campbell, & Ruble, 2013; Sansosti, 2010). Little research is available to document effective RTI practices for children with ASD.

In conceptually reviewing the applicability of the RTI process in the identification of ASD, Hammond et al. (2013) conclude that:

1   Children who have an existing diagnosis of ASD or clear pervasive symptoms should receive an expedited referral to special education and bypass RTI processes;
2   For children identified through a universal screening for symptoms or parent/teacher concerns for ASD, a screening tool should be used.

If the screening indicates possible ASD, a referral to special education should be made and interventions implemented simultaneously;
3 For children suspected of having ASD, a tiered implementation of interventions does not appear appropriate because it may delay identification and the complexity of interventions needed likely does not fit within the RTI model.

Consistent with this, the majority of 117 school psychologists who completed a survey noted that the RTI model is not appropriate for determining eligibility for special education services in the area of ASD (Allen, Robins, & Decker, 2008).

The Office of Special Education and Rehabilitative Services has provided some guidance related to the use of RTI. Federal letters and memorandums have made clear that the RTI processes should not delay a child who is suspected of having a disability from receiving an evaluation to determine eligibility. It states "States and LEAs have an obligation to ensure that evaluations of children suspected of having a disability are not delayed or denied because of implementation of an RTI strategy" (Musgrove, 2011, p. 1). This indicates that if a child is showing clear symptoms of ASD, immediately continuing on to a special education evaluation, perhaps while simultaneously conducting interventions, is appropriate if not most closely aligned with the spirit of the federal law.

Case Study 3

Ruth is a 6-year-old little girl who has never attended school. Ruth's mother comes up to school the week before school starts to enroll her and reports that Ruth "needs extra help." She is unsure if Ruth will be allowed to enroll in school. Ruth is with her mother and the office staff notice some possible developmental delays. The school psychologist is in the building and the office staff asks the school psychologist to come up to meet Ruth.

The school psychologist greets the mother and asks the family to sit down in a nearby conference room to discuss the mother's concerns. Ruth is nonverbal. At this time, she is not able to communicate her needs and wants to others. Her mother starts to cry and hid her face when she admits that Ruth is still wearing diapers. While observing Ruth, you notice that she is preoccupied with a blue straw, flicking it repetitively. She does not initiate any interactions with you or her mother.

- What are possible next steps for the school team?
- What considerations might there be around RTI?
- What messages are important for this mother to hear?

Some states include special education services as the top tier within their RTI process. Within this conceptual framework, the RTI model may be very appropriate for children with ASD. Sansosti (2010) outlined a progressive model of RTI that increased levels of social skills support. Tier 1 included school-wide approaches such as positive behavioral intervention support, character education, and social skills training. Tier 2 included small group interventions such as social skills groups and peer-mediated approaches. Finally, Tier 3 included interventions such as video modeling, social stories, and power cards.

Section 504 of the Rehabilitation Act

Section 504 of the Rehabilitation Act 1973 provides additional protections for children with ASD. In order to be protected by Section 504, a child must have a physical or mental impairment that substantially limits one or more major life activities. Although most children with ASD will likely need special education services, some children may only need some accommodations available through a 504 Plan. Although IDEA entitles children with disabilities to a free and appropriate education, Section 504 protects children with disabilities from discrimination. As such, 504 Plans allow for accommodations to prevent discrimination (Table 7.2);

Table 7.2 Comparison of IDEA versus 504

	IDEA	Section 504
Governing law?	Governed by Individuals with Disabilities Education Act (IDEA). State regulations then implement Part B of IDEA	Governed by Section 504 of the Rehabilitation Act of 1973; oversight by the US Department of Education, Office for Civil Rights (OCR)
Plan name?	Individualized Education Program	Section 504 Plan
Who is eligible?	Only those students who have specified types of educational disabilities and who, because of one or more of those conditions, need special education and related services	Protects all qualified students with disabilities, defined as those people with a physical or mental impairment that substantially limits one or more major life activities
What is provided?	Specialized instruction and accommodations	Accommodations
Funding method?	Local tax base, state, and federal funds	There is no funding source. State and local jurisdictions must provide accommodations under Section 504 if they receive federal financial assistance
Reviewed?	Yearly or more often	Yearly or more often

however, they typically do not provide instructional service. The IDEA definition of disability is more restrictive than the 504 definition of disability. Therefore, all children who fit within the IDEA definition of disability fall within Section 504, but the reverse is not true (Turnbull, Wilcox, & Stowe, 2002).

Table of Cases

Q.W. v Board of Education of Fayette County, Kentucky, 15-5160 (6th Cir., 2015).

References

Allen, R. A., Robins, D. L., & Decker, S. L. (2008). Autism spectrum disorders: Neurobiology and current assessment practices. *Psychology in the Schools*, 45(10), 905–917.

Azad, G. F. & Mandell, D. S. (2016). Concerns of parents and teachers of children with autism in elementary school. *Autism*, 20(4), 435–441. doi:10.1177/1362361315588199.

Azad, G. F., Kim, M., Marcus, S. C., Mandell, D. S., & Sheridan, S. M. (2016). Parent-teacher communication about children with autism spectrum disorder: An examination of collaborative problem-solving. *Psychology in the Schools*, 53(10), 1071–1084. doi:10.1002/pits.21976.

Barton, E. E., Harris, B., Leech, N., Stiff, L., Choi, G., & Joel, T. (2016). An analysis of state autism educational assessment practices and requirements. *Journal of Autism and Developmental Disorders*, 46(3), 737–748. doi:10.1007/s10803-015-2589-0.

Boyce, W. T. & Ellis, B. J. (2005). Biological sensitivity to context: I. An evolutionary–developmental theory of the origins and functions of stress reactivity. *Developmental Psychopathology*, 17(2), 271–301.

Cannon, L., Kenworthy, L., Alexander, K. C., Adler Werner, M., & Gutermuth Anthony, L. (2018). *Unstuck and On Target! An Executive Function Curriculum to Improve Flexibility, Planning, and Organization*, 2nd edn. Baltimore, MD: Brookes Publishing.

Hammond, R. K., Campbell, J. M., & Ruble, L. A. (2013). Considering identification and service provision for students with autism spectrum disorders within the context of response to intervention. *Exceptionality*, 21(1), 34–50. doi:10.1080/09362835.2013.750119.

Laugeson, E. A. (2013). The PEERS Curriculum for School-Based Professionals: Social Skills Training for Adolescents with Autism Spectrum Disorder. New York: Routledge.

Lord, C., Risi, S., DiLavore, P. S., Shulman, C., Thurm, A., & Pickles, A. (2006). Autism from 2 to 9 years of age. *Archives of General Psychiatry*, 63(6), 694–701. doi:10.1001/archpsyc.63.6.694.

Musgrove, M. (2011). A Response to Intervention (RTI) process cannot be used to delay-deny an evaluation for eligibility under the Individuals with Disabilities Education Act (IDEA) [Memorandum to State Directors of Special Education]. Available at: https://www2.ed.gov/policy/speced/guid/idea/memos dcltrs/osep11-07rtimemo.pdf.

Posney, A. (2007). Letter to Catherine Clarke. Available at: https://www2.ed.gov/policy/speced/guid/idea/letters/2007-1/clarke030807disability1q2007.pdf.

Sansosti, F. J. (2010). Teaching social skills to children with autism spectrum disorders using tiers of support: A guide for school-based professionals. *Psychology in the Schools*, 47(3), 257–281.

Stahmer, A. C. & Mandell, D. S. (2007). State infant/toddler program policies for eligibility and services provision for young children with autism. *Administration and Policy in Mental Health and Mental Health Services Research*, 34(1), 29–37. doi:10.1007/s10488-006-0060-4.

Turnbull, H. R., Wilcox, B. L., & Stowe, M. J. (2002). A brief overview of special education law with focus on autism. *Journal of Autism and Developmental Disorders*, 32(5), 479–493. doi:10.1023/a:1020550107880.

Chapter 8

Sharing Assessment Results and Creating a Plan

After the completion of an evaluation for special education eligibility, school psychologists are tasked with sharing the results of these evaluations with teachers, other school professionals (e.g., speech and language pathologists, occupational therapists, social workers), and families in order to help form a plan for students.

Conversations with Parents about Assessment Results

Parents have often been waiting a long time for the moment when a professional will help explain their child's strengths and differences. Although evaluations have traditionally been initiated to help describe a child's weaknesses and form a path forward, it is important also to identify a child's strengths (Tedeschi & Kilmer, 2005). Assessing both a child's strengths and their differences contributes to communicating the value of the child and that the child is more than the sum of weaknesses. This can build trust in the school–family relationship and help families recognize that you are also an advocate for their child. Strengths and interests can become the foundation for the formation of interventions. Starting the assessment session with a description of a child's unique interests, personality, and strengths can set a more positive tone for an assessment results conversation.

Delivering Life-altering Information

Although a feedback session could be seen as merely relaying factual assessment results, conceptualizing the sharing of these results with parents as an intervention can be helpful. When a psychologist has a conversation about results of an autism spectrum disorder (ASD) assessment and interprets the information, families are often hearing information that may change their expectations and view of their child. This can be considered "life-altering information." The quality of the delivery of information about a child's strengths and differences as well as possible eligibility for special education can change how collaborative the eligibility and working relationship between the parent and school will be.

Relatively few school psychologists are explicitly taught how to have conversations about assessment results with families. The practice of delivering this information is typically learned by watching supervisors and mentors as well as the honing of practice over time. School psychologists and eligibility teams are regularly asked to share eligibility-related news to families, communicating for the first time to families that their child has a disability. This information is often perceived as bad news by families. Research indicates that psychologists are often hesitant to share bad news with a family and have received little formal education in delivering bad news (Merker, Hanson, & Poston, 2010). The MUM effect, or the tendency to want to avoid bad news and emphasize positive news, often affects psychologists (Tesser, Rosen, & Batchelor, 1972). Sharing bad news with a family can cause significant anxiety (Merker et al., 2010). School psychologists may be anxious that they will be blamed for the bad news, will be in a negative mood themselves after sharing the news, will emotionally upset the parents, or might be wrong in their interpretation of the results (Merker et al., 2010). It may be helpful to remember that, although the school psychologist is delivering the bad news, they are not the cause of the child's disability.

Guidelines for Sharing Assessment Results

There are no clear guidelines for sharing assessment results and eligibility information in the context of psychological assessment; however, models adopted from pediatric, medical settings can be beneficial. The SPIKE model from the Pediatric Hospital Guidelines for Sharing Life-Altering

Table 8.1 SPIKE model from the "Pediatric hospital guidelines for sharing life-altering information"

S – Setting	Who will be there, minimize distractions, which family members are present, team on the same page
P – Perceptions	What does the family already know, correct misperceptions
I – Involvement	Family-centered, confirm agenda of meeting, encourage questions, consider culture of family
K – Knowledge	Connect with previous information, use key points, use visual aids, avoid jargon, emphasize positive findings when possible, discuss possible outcomes
E – Empathize	Validate feelings of family, clarify what they are worried about
S – Strategy, Summary, Self-reflection	Check if family is ready to discuss plan, discuss next steps and encourage family participation, balance hope/realism, reflect on the process yourself

Information is one such model (Wolfe et al., 2014). The model focuses on considering the Setting, Perceptions, Involvement, Knowledge, Empathize, and Strategy/Summary.

Setting

In addressing the setting, attempt to locate a room and find a quiet location with enough chairs to include relevant family and family friends. Have tissues available. Time is precious within the school system, but, if at all possible, meet with the family in private before sharing assessment results in the context of an eligibility meeting. This may be particularly important when the information will likely result in an ASD eligibility rather than a higher incidence disability (e.g., learning disability). Learning that their child is demonstrating symptoms of an ASD is personal and emotional. Having to first hear the information in a room full of strangers can be overwhelming and not allow the family to fully digest the information. Often a family member will attend a feedback session alone; however, it is helpful to invite the family member to include a partner, relative, or family friend. Find out how each adult present is related to the child.

Perception

Assess the family's current perceptions and understandings of ASD. It can be helpful to probe if the family knows anyone with ASD because their experience with this individual may heavily influence their understanding of the results you share. Parents and professionals often have significant differences in understanding the causes of ASD (Fischbach et al., 2016). Levy et al. (2003) provide several questions that can be used to understand a family's beliefs about ASD causes, treatment, and expectations:

1. What did you call your child's problem before it was diagnosed?
2. What do you think caused it?
3. Why do you think it started when it did?
4. What do you think autism does? How does it work?
5. How severe is it? Will it have a short or long course?
6. What are the chief problems you child's autism has caused?
7. What do you fear most about it? and
8. What kind of treatment do you think your child should receive? What do you expect from this treatment?

(Levy et al., 2003, p. 422)

Beliefs related to the causes of ASD can vary widely based on a family's socioeconomic status, culture, and worldview. Families may emphasize biomedical or preternatural/supernatural causes (Danseco, 1997; Gona et al., 2015). If the family focuses on biomedical genetic reasons for ASD, they may feel responsible for passing on "negative genes," emphasizing hereditary versus *de novo* genetic changes. Families may also blame themselves for their child's autism due to choices they have made that affect the child's social environment (e.g., lack of preschool, lack of staying home with the child) or biomedical environment (e.g., smoking during pregnancy, infections, maternal malnutrition, vaccinating their child). Some may blame others for their child's ASD (e.g., obstetrician's failures).

Related to spirituality, parents, particularly mothers, may feel responsible for their child's ASD whether due to a curse, misbalanced yin/yang, or spiritual sin on their own part. Alternatively, spiritual beliefs may cause families to feel that their child with ASD has equal value as a neurotypical children or a higher spiritual calling (Hebert & Koulouglioti, 2010). Families may feel that having a child with ASD is a blessing from God which provides an opportunity to sacrifice themselves to serve their child (Ennis-Cole, Durodoye, & Harris, 2013).

Different families vary in their beliefs related to whether ASD is lifelong or temporary, whether treatment can change a child's functioning, whether the family can influence the child's development, or whether ASD is a mystery. Lower-income and less educated families may believe that ASD is a mystery and feel they do not have the power to affect the severity of their child's symptoms (Zuckerman et al., 2015). In addition, families from cultural minorities may be more likely to believe that ASD is a temporary condition (Zuckerman et al., 2015).

Understanding family's beliefs can provide opportunities to provide alternative, evidenced-based theories of ASD causation, anticipate possible skepticism about recommended treatments, and encourage the family to rely on aspects of their belief system for social support. When school psychologists do not initiate conversations about beliefs around ASD, there are more likely to be unrecognized conflicts between the school's understanding of ASD and necessary intervention and the family's understanding (Danseco, 1997). An opportunity for collaboration between the family and school is missed.

Involvement

Throughout the feedback, encourage family involvement and allow for questions. The time should be a conversation in which both parties share information and build a common understanding of the child. Check for parents' understanding often, leave pauses in your speech to allow them to interject, and avoid a prolonged monologue. While sharing results, check to see if the results you share are consistent with some of the strengths and differences that the parents have noticed about their child.

Acknowledge the parents' facial expressions and body language, directly addressing them when appropriate. For example, if parents pull back and cross their arms when you tell them their child is demonstrating symptoms consistent with an ASD, ask, "Is what I'm telling you different from what you were expecting?"

Parents often ask about future outcomes or future hopes for their child. It should be acknowledged that the parents' hopes and despairs for themselves can be related to their child's future, a concept referred to as vicarious futurity (Hebert & Koulouglioti, 2010). For example, a parent may be looking forward to having conversations over tea parties with her daughter and her daughter is nonverbal. This may be a loss not only for the child, but also for the parent.

Relatively little information is available about outcomes for very young children with ASD, so it can be helpful to communicate that research indicates factors such as an early age of diagnosis, functional communication by age five years, strong adaptive skills, and average nonverbal abilities are related to more positive outcomes in children with ASD (Kanne et al., 2011; Moulton et al., 2016; Wodka, Mathy, & Kalb, 2013). Emphasizing the types of empirically supported intervention that may give most support to increasing communication, and social and adaptive skills can be a helpful in this discussion. For older children, discussing the importance of transitioning to adult life and cultivating the needed adaptive skills is an important focus.

Knowledge

While providing information to families, attempt to minimize jargon, use visual aids, and speak at a level the family can understand. Relatively little guidance is available for practitioners regarding how to share information about the presence of ASD symptoms with caregivers. Monteiro (2010, 2016, 2018) provides the most comprehensive conversational method. She has developed a visual system to guide evaluators through the process of individualizing the autism diagnostic conversation with parents and caregivers. Her descriptive triangle emphasizes laying out the individual's pattern of differences in development or differences in brain style in the three core areas of: Language and communication, social relationships and emotions, and sensory use and interests. The terminology of sensory use and interests is used to replace the negative language used in the ASD criteria of restricted interests and repetitive behaviors. Descriptive language is used to identify strengths and differences in each of the three areas. Combining the descriptive language with the visual triangle when talking with families is a powerful way to both individualize the diagnosis and state the pattern of differences in accessible language. The use of the visual system allows families and evaluators to come to consensus about

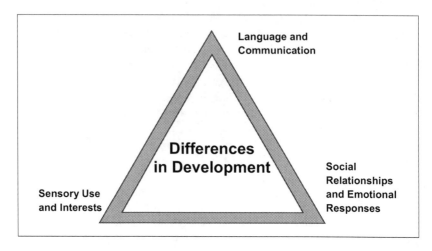

Figure 8.1 Monteiro's descriptive triangle
(Used with permission from Marilyn Monteiro.)

the individual's behavioral profile before introducing the diagnostic term of Autism Spectrum Disorder. Physically drawing the Descriptive Triangle while discussing the individual's pattern of strengths and differences in each of the key areas provides families with the experience of a shared perspective on their unique child instead of emphasizing the diagnostic term and assuming a shared understanding of that term as it relates to the individual. The diagnostic term ASD makes more sense to families when presented after the triangle of the individual's pattern of strengths and differences has been laid out in the conversational format. Using the triangle framework helps to make abstract symptoms more accessible and gives families a tangible representation of the conversation to take with them.

Within the school setting, it can be delicate and difficult to make a clear statement about the presence of symptoms consistent with ASD without predetermining a child's eligibility; however, making a clear statement that a child meets eligibility criteria for an ASD is important. At some point during the eligibility process the family needs to hear, "Your child qualifies for special education in the area of Autism Spectrum Disorder." After making this statement, pause. Allow a few seconds to pass. Give the family a moment to let this information sink in. Ask them if this is a surprise or what they were expecting.

Empathize

Throughout the feedback session, aim to validate the family's feelings and clarify their concerns. This can include addressing misinformation about the causes of ASD and potential blame that the family feels. Families may bring up the fear of stigma related to ASD. Many families anticipate experiencing stigma, particularly feelings of rejection and exclusion (Kinnear et al., 2016). During the process, it is important to remember the many feelings and processes that can be associated with grief, including denial, bargaining, anger, sadness, and acceptance (Kübler-Ross, 2009). Although feelings of grief are common, some families experience a sense of relief after looking for answers about their child's functioning. Validating this feeling can also be important for parents. Sometimes, when two family members are present, one family member is more comfortable in beginning a conversation about the plan of what to do, whereas the other is still digesting the news that their child has an ASD. Acknowledging and educating parents that people react differently to news of ASD and that multiple responses are valid, can provide space for family members to grieve differently and avoid some conflict. Similarly, families may be anticipating how they will share the news with family members who are not present. Finally, although parents may direct their feelings of anger toward the school staff, remembering that the parent is experiencing grief can help diffuse your own negative reaction and find common ground to continue the special education process.

Talking with Families 1

The experience of having a child with ASD often creates significant stress. Furthermore, having a child with a disability often places a stress on marriages. Wherever possible, address stress with the family. Encourage the caretakers to engage in self-care, taking care of their own physical, mental, social, and spiritual health. A child's family is one of the child's greatest assets.

Sometimes using the following illustration can be helpful:

> When you fly on an airplane, you are told, "If there is a sudden change in air pressure, oxygen masks will fall from the ceiling. If a child is seated next to you, put on your own mask before helping to put the mask on the child." Similarly, your child needs you to be healthy in order to take care of them.

Families often need to be reminded and given "permission" to consider the functioning of the entire family when making decisions about their child's private intervention services. In our society which often emphasizes individual needs, parents of children with special needs can feel guilty if they do not engage their child in every available intervention.

Strategy and Summary

After discussing the results, check to see if the family is ready to discuss the next steps and balance hope/realism. The IEP provides a structured means to form a strategy and plan for a student. Finally, although caring for a family through the assessment process is very important, self-care for the professional should not be forgotten. It is not easy to deliver "bad news" regularly. Recognize your own feelings and symptoms of burnout. Seek out support from peers. Engage in self-care activities.

Written Reports

Hopefully, assessment results are first communicated to a family through a conversation about a child's strengths and differences; however, there is typically also a written report that communicates the same information. The National Association of School Psychologists produced a three-part series on writing psychoeducational reports that outlined some of the key components of reports and recommendations for facilitating their usefulness (Lichtenstein, 2013). In discussing the purposes of evaluations within school systems, the document asserts:

A key assumption concerns that most important purposes of an evaluation, namely:

- To provide an accurate and in-depth description of the child's functioning, capabilities, needs, and situational challenges.
- To provide diagnostic conclusions that focus intervention efforts and determine the range of available options (e.g., special education eligibility); and, most important,
- To provide insights and recommendations that improve the functioning and well-being of the child.

Reports should be written in language that parents and school professionals can understand. Therefore, terms like echolalia, neologisms, social reciprocity, joint attention, stereotyped behaviors, visual peering, self-stimulating behavior, and stereotyped interests should be defined in understandable language if used at all. Providing a description or examples of a child's behavior that meet eligibility criteria are more helpful than technical wording.

> ### Case Study 1
>
> Compare these two descriptions of 8-year-old Marc's behavior that could appear in a psychological report. Which description would provide an IEP team with more information to inform educational goals for Marc?

> **Marc Description 1**
>
> Marc exhibits problems with joint social reciprocity and use of nonverbal communication. His language often includes stereotyped language and has an unusual intonation. Further, he demonstrates stereotyped hand behaviors, stereotyped interests, and visual peering.
>
> **Marc Description 2**
>
> Marc demonstrates differences in his social interactions. He has an expertise related to the solar system. He loves sharing facts about the solar system, but sometimes he changes the subject to the solar system when talking with his peers. He has trouble understanding others' personal space and signals that they want to talk about something else. When he speaks, he often relies on familiar, adult-like phrases. For example, he might say, "On the other hand," or "Well, actually." When saying these phrases, the tone of his voice tends to have a sing-song quality. Marc also tends to subtly tense and wiggle his fingers when he is excited or distressed. He is also very detailed oriented and will notice small visual differences in objects, studying them closely.
>
> **Kayla Description**
>
> How could this description of a 4-year-old Kayla be rewritten to be more parent and teacher-friendly?
>
> Kayla struggles to engage in joint attention and coordinate eye contact with verbal and nonverbal communication. She exhibits stereotyped behaviors, auditory sensory-seeking behaviors, and a routine orientation.

Although it can be tempting to include a long list of recommendations, this can be overwhelming for parents and teachers alike. Although only an IEP team can determine a child's goals, accommodations, and placement, formal reports can offer ideas or possible suggestions when written with tentative language (e.g., Johnny may benefit from accommodations such as visual schedules and social stories). Including a few sample ideas for areas of focus for IEP goals can be helpful as well. These goals should focus on children's social communication, emotional/behavioral regulation, and adaptive skills.

Coordinating with Multidisciplinary Staff

The determination of special education eligibility as outlined in Chapter 7 requires the participation of many stakeholders. Although sharing the results of the psychological evaluation are particularly important for parents, other staff members who care about the child are often anxious to hear the results. In addition, other members of the multidisciplinary team such as speech and language pathologists, occupational therapists, special education teachers, behavioral specialists, nurses, and social workers may be involved. These team members can provide valuable information to inform your evaluation and are also important to communicate assessment results to. It is beneficial to incorporate multidiciplinary results before an eligibility meeting. At the least, it is important to share assessment results with other professionals before meeting with parents in order to reconcile any possible discrepancies in the data across stakeholders.

Creating the Initial Individualized Education Program

After eligibility is established, the initial IEP is created. A child's current functioning informs individual goals. Goals then help determine the types of support and educational environment a child will need. Collaboration across school psychologists, speech and language pathologists, occupational therapists, social workers, general education teachers, special education teachers, and parents is critical in the development of an IEP. Incorporating parents into this process is critical. Taking a couple of minutes to educate parents about the format and general flow (e.g., current functioning, goals, accommodations, and placement) of the IEP can help them participate in the meeting. Asking parents what one or two areas they would like to see progress can be a way to incorporate parents in the process and ensure the IEP is addressing the areas of greatest need for a child. For example, parents are often very concerned when their four year old is not toilet trained because it is not only time-consuming, but also financially expensive.

Goal Creation

Although schools are generally very good at considering academic goals, goals related to key areas of deficit for children with ASD, namely a child's social communication, emotional–behavioral regulation, and adaptive skills goals, are sometimes not as prominent in IEPs. Social communication goals need to focus on increasing the child's ability to functionally communicate needs and wants, interact with others, and engage in reciprocal interactions. Related to adaptive functioning, skills associated with personal care, safety, and community use are important. For emotional regulation goals, skills associated with transitioning between tasks/topics, identifying and relating emotions appropriately, and engaging in socially appropriate calming strategies may be particularly needed for children with ASD. The SCERTS model provides resources for conceptualizing students' social communication and emotional regulation needs and related goals (Prizant et al., 2006).

Table 8.2 Sample areas of focus for IEP goals and supportive aids

Social communication

- Student will use convention gestures such as pointing and giving
- Student will use eye contact in coordination with vocalization or gesture to make a request
- Student will make a request between two offered toys or foods
- Student will request help with language
- Student will use a variety of word combinations
- Student will take three turns with an adult
- Student will take three turns with a peer
- Student will engage in pretend play with a peer
- Student will invite a peer to play
- Student will start a conversation of interest to others
- Student will use appropriate body proximity when talking with others
- Student will initiate play dates
- Student will appropriately follow group consensus

Adaptive skills

- Student will notify adult when their diaper is wet
- Student will use utensils when eating
- Student will independently use the bathroom
- Student will dress themselves
- Student will wash their hands independently
- Student will navigate the school building independently
- Student will demonstrate when and how to call 911
- Student will distinguish between stranger and known person
- Student will prepare simple meals
- Student will show appropriate use and safety knowledge related to the internet
- Student will receive feedback in the workplace
- Student will use public transportation

Emotional regulation

- Student will transition between work stations with visual cues
- Student will calmly transition between the playground and classroom
- Student will independently follow a multi-task activity with picture cues
- Student will use pictures or words to express emotion
- Student will express anger appropriately
- Student will use self-talk to adjust to a change in school routine
- Student will express disagreement appropriately
- Student will self-advocate to ask for breaks

Supportive aids provided by school staff

- Visual cue
- Visual schedule
- Sensory supports
- Picture communication
- Social story
- Timers
- Video modeling

Some goals adapted from Prizant et al. (2006).

Goals should be written using a SMART format, meaning they should be specific, measurable, achievable, relevant, and timely. An "S," representing supportive aids, can be added to create SMARTS in order to remind educators that children with ASD will needed to be provided with supports to reach their goals. So, if the concern is toilet training, the goal might be: William will request to use the bathroom using a teacher created visual cue card three out of five times by three months from today.

When litigious situations arise concerning on the autism spectrum, it is often related to issues with IEP content and implementation (White et al., 2014). It is likely that goals will be of increasing importance following the *Endrew F v. Douglas County School District RE-1* (2017) case. This case involved a child with ASD who made little progress on his IEP goals. The parents argued that Endrew was not being provided a free and appropriate education, whereas the school held that Endrew only had the right to a *de minimis*, or minimal, benefit from his IEP. Previously, the *Board of Ed. of Hendrick Hudson Central School Dist., Westchester Cty v. Rowley* (1982) set the standard that entitled a child to an IEP that was "reasonably calculated to enable the child to receive educational benefits." This has often been seen to require that children with an IEP must make only minimal progress. In the *Endrew F* case, Chief Justice John G. Roberts asserted that "The IDEA demands more. It requires an educational program reasonably calculated to enable a child to make progress appropriate in light of the child's circumstances." This requires substantially more than the previous standard set in the *Rowley* case. The *Endrew* case asserted that if it is not reasonable for a child to be fully integrated in a general education classroom and make progress at a grade-level expectations:

> His IEP need not aim for grade-level advancement. But his educational program must be appropriately ambitious in light of his circumstances, just as advancement from grade to grade is appropriately ambitious for most children in the regular classroom. The goals may differ, but every child should have the chance to meet challenging objectives.
> (*Endrew F v. Douglas County School District RE-1* [2017])

Educational Placement

Children's educational placement should be driven by their needs as expressed through their goals. As children's goals vary from the general curriculum and become more numerous, children are more likely to need a more restrictive environment. The balance between meeting a child's needs and providing the most inclusive environment can be difficult. In addition, children's needs may shift over time, requiring different environmental and instructional supports. However, some research indicates that early educational placement decisions continue throughout a child's educational progression (White et al., 2007). There is no clear research to indicate which educational environment is best for which children, which may be why the placement of children with ASD is often an area of contention between schools and families (Burke & Goldman, 2015).

Related to current practices, children with lower cognitive abilities, weaker communication abilities, more severe ASD symptoms, greater disruptive behaviors, and lower executive functioning skills are more likely to be placed in more restrictive environments (Delmolino & Harris, 2012; White et al., 2007). In contrast, children's social and adaptive deficits have not been shown to be associated with IEP decisions for placement in a more restrictive environment (White et al., 2007). Children with ASD are more likely to receive speech and occupational therapy than behavioral management programming and mental health services (Wei et al., 2014). In general, as students age, they receive fewer special education services with the exception of high school students who receive more mental health support (Wei et al., 2014).

Although a child's characteristics should be associated with educational placement, contextual factors such as the state in which the child resides are associated with placement decisions (Kurth, 2015). As a result, the role of individual school, district, and regional policies and procedures may influence children's educational placements.

IEP committees often consider the value that socially skilled peers may provide for a child with ASD in a general education classroom. However, there is no clear consensus on which children benefit from greater inclusion. There is some indication that boys and girls may fare differently within inclusive classrooms. For girls, larger general education classrooms may be beneficial to their social connectedness to peers; however, smaller general education classrooms may be better for boys (Anderson et al. 2016). Furthermore, children initially placed in general education settings, and then later moved to more restrictive special education settings, show a greater decrease in social and adaptive skills than peers initially placed in more restrictive environments (White et al., 2007). This indicates that general education settings may sometimes cause a student to develop social and adaptive skills at a slower rate than if he or she were in a more restrictive environment that focused on more direct instruction of these skills.

Interventions

Although there is not clear guidance on which education environments are most beneficial for which children with ASD, there are a number of evidence-based interventions that support improvement in the core

Table 8.3 Interventions identified by the National Autism Center as falling into the established level of evidence

The following interventions have been identified as falling into the Established level of evidence by the National Autism Center (2015):
- Behavioral interventions
- Cognitive–behavioral intervention package
- Comprehensive behavioral treatment for young children
- Language training (production)
- Modeling
- Natural teaching strategies
- Parent training
- Peer training package
- Pivotal response training
- Schedules
- Scripting
- Self-management
- Social skills package
- Story-based intervention

symptoms of ASD. These interventions can be used to support students in reaching their IEP goals. Through consultation, school psychologists can guide educators in selecting pedagogical methods that are evidence based. The National Autism Center (www.nationalautismcenter.org) and the Association for Science in Autism Treatment (www.asatonline.org) both provide syntheses of research findings and identify interventions that have a strong evidence base as well as those with weaker evidence. Evidence-based therapies tend to rely on applied behavioral analysis (ABA) to increase behaviors and teach new behaviors as well as early intensive behavioral interventions for preschool children.

Currently, there is little to no evidence supporting the use of nutritional supplements or dietary interventions, such as omega-3 and gluten-/casein-free diets, to treat symptoms associated with ASD (Sathe et al., 2017). Furthermore, the evidence to support therapies associated with sensory challenges, such as sensory integration therapy or auditory integration therapy, is limited (National Autism Center, 2015; Weitlauf et al., 2017). Some therapies may produce short-term results; however, the durability of these therapies has not yet been demonstrated.

Transitions

As the increasing number of children identified as having ASD age and begin to transition out of school, transition planning will become an increasingly important area of focus. This is particularly true because the current rates of postsecondary education and employment are very low for individuals with ASD. Although federal law does not require IEP teams to begin transition planning until the year a student turns 16 years old, transition planning likely needs to begin earlier. The National Technical Assistance Center on Transition (https://transitionta.org/researchpractices) outlines evidence-based and research-based practices that support successful transitions for students. Factors that support successful transitions include paid or unpaid work experience, employment preparation, family involvement, inclusion in general education, social skills training, daily living skills, self-determination skills training, and community/agency collaboration.

As state educational services come to an end, state Vocational Rehabilitation (VR) programs begin to provide services for some individuals with ASD. State VR programs help people with disabilities achieve independence and meaningful employment. The Rehabilitation Act of 1973 guides and funds VR programs. In order to be eligible for VR services, an individual must (1) have a physical or mental impairment that constitutes or results in a substantial impediment to employment, and (2) require VR services to prepare for, secure, retain, advance in, or regain employment. Priority must be given to serving individuals with the most significant disabilities if a state is unable to serve all eligible individuals.

A strength-based approach can facilitate transition planning. Strengths in areas such as visuospatial skills, creativity, attention to detail, and memory can be assets for individuals with ASD (Mahdi et al., 2018). In addition, the intense interests of individuals with ASD may serve as a career path. Sensory sensitivities can also be a strength. For example, individuals with ASD may be particularly perceptive to differences in lighting, sound, and taste. This acute perception may be helpful in careers related to lighting and sound production, as well as social activities such as food and drink tasting. Finally, personal characteristics such as a direct communication style and strong sense of justice can contribute to workplace success in careers related to technical writing and advocacy work.

Table of Cases

Board of Ed. of Hendrick Hudson Central School Dist., Westchester Cty v. Rowley, No. 80-1002 458 (U.S. 176, 1982).
Endrew F. v. Douglas County School District RE-1, No. 580 (Supreme Court of the United States 2017).

References

Anderson, A., Locke, J., Kretzmann, M., & Kasari, C. (2016). Social network analysis of children with autism spectrum disorder: Predictors of fragmentation and connectivity in elementary school classrooms. *Autism*, 20(6), 700–709. doi:doi:10.1177/1362361315603568

Burke, M. & Goldman, S. (2015). Identifying the associated factors of mediation and due process in families of students with Autism Spectrum Disorder. *Journal of Autism & Developmental Disorders*, 45(5), 1345–1353. doi:10.1007/s10803-014-2294-4.

Danseco, E. R. (1997). Parental beliefs on childhood disability: Insights on culture, child development and intervention. *International Journal of Disability, Development and Education*, 44(1), 41–52. doi:10.1080/0156655970440104.

Delmolino, L. & Harris, S. (2012). Matching children on the autism spectrum to classrooms: A guide for parents and professionals. *Journal of Autism & Developmental Disorders*, 42(6), 1197–1204. doi:10.1007/s10803-011-1298-6.

Ennis-Cole, D., Durodoye, B. A., & Harris, H. L. (2013). The impact of culture on Autism diagnosis and treatment: Considerations for counselors and other professionals. *Family Journal*, 21(3), 279–287. doi:10.1177/1066480713476834

Fischbach, R. L., Harris, M. J., Ballan, M. S., Fischbach, G. D., & Link, B. G. (2016). Is there concordance in attitudes and beliefs between parents and scientists about autism spectrum disorder? *Autism*, 20(3), 353–363. doi:10.1177/1362361315585310

Gona, J. K., Newton, C. R., Rimba, K., Mapenzi, R., Kihara, M., Van de Vijver, F. J. R., & Abubakar, A. (2015). Parents' and professionals' perceptions on causes and treatment options for autism spectrum disorders (ASD) in a multicultural context on the Kenyan coast. *PLoS One*, 10(8), 1–13. doi:10.1371/journal.pone.0132729.

Hebert, E. B. & Koulouglioti, C. (2010). Parental beliefs about cause and course of their child's Autism and outcomes of their beliefs: A review of the literature. *Issues in Comprehensive Pediatric Nursing*, 33(3), 149–163. doi:10.3109/01460862.2010.498331.

Kanne, S. M., Gerber, A. J., Quirmbach, L. N., Sparrow, S. S., Cicchetti, D. V., & Saulnier, C. A. (2011). The role of adaptive behavior in autism spectrum disorders: Implications for functional outcome. *Journal of Autism & Developmental Disorders*, 41(8), 1007–1018. doi:10.1007/s10803-010-1126-4.

Kinnear, S., Link, B., Ballan, M., & Fischbach, R. (2016). Understanding the experience of stigma for parents of children with autism spectrum disorder and the role stigma plays in families' lives. *Journal of Autism & Developmental Disorders*, 46(3), 942–953. doi:10.1007/s10803-015-2637-9.

Kübler-Ross, E. (2009). *On death and Dying: What the dying have to teach doctors, nurses, clergy and their own families*. Available at: EBSCOhost http://search.ebscohost.com/login.aspx?direct=true&scope=site&db=nlebk&db=nlabk&AN=236501; MyiLibrary: www.myilibrary.com?id=175373

Kurth, J. A. (2015). Educational placement of students with autism. *Focus on Autism & Other Developmental Disabilities*, 30(4), 249–256. doi:10.1177/1088357614547891.

Levy, S. E., Mandell, D. S., Merhar, S., Ittenbach, R. F., & Pinto-Martin, J. A. (2003). Use of complementary and alternative medicine among children recently diagnosed with autistic spectrum disorder. *Journal of Developmental and Behavioral Pediatrics*, 24(6), 418–423.

Lichtenstein, R. (2013). Psychoeducational reports that matter: A consumer-responsive approach. *Communique*, 42(3). Available at: www.nasponline.org/

publications/periodicals/communique/issues/volume-42-issue-3/writing-psychoeducational-reports-that-matter.

Mahdi, S., Albertowski, K., Almodayfer, O., Arsenopoulou, V., Carucci, S., Dias, J. C., et al. (2018). An international clinical study of ability and disability in Autism Spectrum Disorder using the WHO-ICF framework. *Journal of Autism and Developmental Disorders*, 48(6), 2148–2163. doi:10.1007/s10803-018-3482-4.

Merker, B. M., Hanson, W. E., & Poston, J. M. (2010). National survey of psychologists' training and practice in breaking bad news: a mixed methods study of the MUM effect. *Journal of Clinical Psychology In Medical Settings*, 17(3), 211–219. doi:10.1007/s10880-010-9197-0.

Moulton, E., Barton, M., Robins, D. L., Abrams, D. N., & Fein, D. (2016). Early characteristics of children with ASD who demonstrate optimal progress between age two and four. *Journal of Autism and Developmental Disorders*, 46(6), 2160–2173. doi:10.1007/s10803-016-2745-1.

Monteiro, M. J. (2010). *Autism Conversations: Evaluating Children on the Autism Spectrum through Authentic Conversations*. Los Angeles, CA: Western Psychological Services.

Monteiro, M. J. (2016). *Family Therapy and the Autism Spectrum: Autism Conversations in Narrative Practice*. New York: Routledge.

Monteiro, M. J. & Stegall, S. (2018). *Monteiro Interview Guidelines for Diagnosing the Autism Spectrum – 2*. Los Angeles, CA: Western Psychological Services.

National Autism Center (2015). *Findings and Conclusions: National standards project, Phase 2*. Randolph, MA: National Autism Center.

Prizant, B. M., Wetherby, A. M., Rubin, E., Laurent, A. C., & Rydell, P. J. (2006). *The SCERTS Model*. Baltimore: Brookes Publishing.

Sathe, N., Andrews, J. C., McPheeters, M. L., & Warren, Z. E. (2017). Nutritional and dietary interventions for autism spectrum disorder: A systematic review. *Pediatrics*, 139(6), ii. doi:10.1542/peds.2017-0346.

Tedeschi, R. G. & Kilmer, R. P. (2005). Assessing strengths, resilience, and growth to guide clinical interventions. *Professional Psychology: Research and Practice*, 36(3), 230–237. doi:10.1037/0735-7028.36.3.230.

Tesser, A., Rosen, S., & Batchelor, T. R. (1972). Some message variables and the MUM Effect. *Journal of Personality*, 40(1), 88–103. doi:10.1111/1467-6494.ep8969017.

Wei, X., Wagner, M., Christiano, E. R. A., Shattuck, P., & Yu, J. W. (2014). Special education services received by students with autism spectrum disorders from preschool through high school. *Journal of Special Education*, 48(3), 167–179. doi:10.1177/0022466913483576.

Weitlauf, A. S., Sathe, N., McPheeters, M. L., & Warren, Z. E. (2017). Interventions targeting sensory challenges in autism spectrum disorder: A systematic review. *Pediatrics*, 139(6), ii. doi:10.1542/peds.2017-0347.

White, S. E. (2014). Special education complaints filed by parents of students with autism spectrum disorders in the midwestern United States. *Focus on Autism & Other Developmental Disabilities*, 29(2), 80–87. doi:10.1177/1088357613478830.

White, S. W., Scahill, L., Klin, A., Koenig, K., & Volkmar, F. R. (2007). Educational placements and service use patterns of individuals with autism spectrum disorders. *Journal of Autism & Developmental Disorders*, 37(8), 1403–1412. doi:10.1007/s10803-006-0281-0.

Wodka, E. L., Mathy, P., & Kalb, L. (2013). Predictors of phrase and fluent speech in children with autism and severe language delay. *Pediatrics*, 131(4), e1128–e1134. doi:10.1542/peds.2012-2221

Wolfe, A. D., Frierdich, S. A., Wish, J., Kilgore-Carlin, J., Plotkin, J. A., & Hoover-Regan, M. (2014). Sharing life-altering information: Development of pediatric hospital guidelines and team training. *Journal of Palliative Medicine*, 17(9), 1011–1018. doi:10.1089/jpm.2013.0620.

Zuckerman, K. E., Lindly, O. J., Sinche, B. K., & Nicolaidis, C. (2015). Parent health beliefs, social determinants of health, and child health services utilization among U.S. school-age children with autism. *Journal of Developmental & Behavioral Pediatrics*, 36(3), 146–157. doi:10.1097/DBP.0000000000000136.

Index

22q11.2 deletion 29
academic assessment 94–95
Achenbach System of Empirically Based Assessment 88
adaptive functioning 86–87: assessment 86; patterns 86
Adaptive Behavior Assessment System, 3rd edn (ABAS-3) 86
adverse impact 118
age of diagnosis 45, 120: cognitive ability 45; first born child 45; race and ethnicity 46
aggressive behavior 65–66
Angelman's syndrome 28
anxiety disorder 62–63
Asperger, Hans 7
Attention-deficit Hyperactivity Disorder 63–64
Autism Diagnostic Observation Schedule, 2nd edn (ADOS-2) 84–85
Autism Navigator 5
Autism Spectrum Disorders (ASD): core features 4–6; course 12–16; medical and educational identification 6–7; rates 11–12; *see also* history
Autism Spectrum Disorder special education eligibility 117; educational performance 118
Autism Spectrum Rating Scale (ASRS) 87

Bayley Scales of Infant and Toddler Development, 3rd edn (Bayley-III) 82
Behavior Assessment System for Children, 3rd edn (BASC-3) 88
Behavior Rating Inventory of Executive Functions, 2nd edn (BRIEF-2) 97
behavioral interventions 45, 67–68, 141–142
Berry–Buktenica Test of Visual Motor Integration, 6th edn 97
bilingual children: intervention 50; language development in ASD 47–48, 49; parental experiences 48; *see also* age of diagnosis
Bleuler, Eugen 7
Board of Ed. of Hendrick Hudson Central School Dist., Westchester Cty v. Rowley 140

California Verbal Learning Test, Children's version 97
causes of ASD: gene-environment interaction 24–25; *see also* environmental factors and genetic factors
CHARGE syndrome 28
chemical Exposure 35–37
Childhood Autism Rating Scale, 2nd edn (CARS-2) 85
Children's Communication Checklist 90
Clinical Evaluation of Language Fundamentals, 5th edn (CELF-5) 90
cognitive abilities 81–83, 95: patterns 83; relation to academic abilities 95; *see also* age of identification
cognitive assessment 81–83
cognitive–behavioral intervention package 63, 142
Cohen's syndrome 28

Communication and Symbolic Behavior scales, Developmental profile: Infant-Toddler Checklist 76
Comprehensive Assessment of Spoken Language, 2nd edn (CASL-2) 90
comprehensive diagnostic assessment 78
Comprehensive Test of Nonverbal Intelligence, 2nd edn (CTONI-2) 83
Comprehensive Test of Phonological Processing, 2nd edn (CTOPP-2) 97
Conners Early Childhood Scale 88
Cornelia de Lange syndrome 28
cultural differences: perceptions of ASD 131–132; see also age of identification

depression 63
developmental assessment 81–82
Developmental Delay special education eligibility see Significant Developmental Delay special education eligibility
Diagnostic and Statistical Manual, 5th edition (DSM-5) 10
Differential Ability Scale, 2nd edn (DAS-2) 82, 83, 96
DiGeorge's syndrome 29
direct play assessment 83–86
diverse populations 45
Down's syndrome 28
dysmorphic features 31

ear infections 60
early identification of ASD 44, 119
early intervention 45
early symptoms 12
elopement 69
Endrew F v. Douglas County School District RE-1 140
environmental risk and protective factors 33–38: environmental and chemical exposure 35; folic acid 34; maternal antidepressant use 38; maternal substance use 37–38; parental age 33; pregnancy and birth 34–35; protective intervention 38
executive functioning 96

feeding 68–69
Feifer Assessment of Math (FAM) 97
Feifer Assessment of Reading (FAR) 97
First Words Project 5
food allergies 60
Fragile X syndrome 28
Frankl, George 9

gastrointestinal symptoms 60
genetic differences: *de novo* 29; disorders associated with ASD 28–29; dysmorphia 31; familial 29–30; genotype 26; rates 26; risk factors 27
genetic testing 26, 32–33: microarray 27; Whole Exome Sequencing 27; Whole Genome Sequencing 27
giftedness 61–62
girls with ASD 50–52: assessment 52; differences in rates from boys 49–51; presentation 51–52; rates of diagnosis 50; young women 52–53

hearing impairment 59–60
history of ASD: medical 7–9; educational history 10; educational history 8; neurodiversity movement 10–11

IDEA 115: history 10; Part B Eligibility 117–119; Part C Eligibility 116–117, 119
Individualized Education Program: early transition services 119; educational placement 140–141; goal creation 138–139; initial development 138; intervention 142; *see also* Autism Spectrum Disorder special education eligibility; *see also* transition planning
Individualized Family Service Plan 117
infants and toddlers with disabilities 116
intellectual disability 61
International Classification of Diseases, 10th edn (ICD-10) 9
interventions 141–142

Kanner, Leo 9
Kaufman Assessment Battery for Children, 2nd edn (KABC-2) 83, 96
Kaufman Test of Educational Achievement, 3rd edn (KTEA-3) 95

language functioning: assessment 89–90; pragmatic language 89; receptive and expressive language patterns 82
language production training 142
lead exposure 35
Learn the Signs 5
Leiter International Performance Scale, 3rd edn 83
long-term retrieval 96

math skills 101–103; calculation 102; early numeracy 102; hypercalculia 102; problem solving 103
math calculation 102
math problem solving 103
medical comorbidities 58–60
medical evaluation 89: EEG 89; MRI 89
mercury exposure 35
Mills v Board of Education, District of Columbia 10
modeling 142
Modified Checklist for Autism in Toddlers, Revised 78
Monteiro Interview Guidelines for Diagnosing the Autism Spectrum 86
Monteiro Triangle 133–134
Mullen Scales of Early Learning 82
multidisciplinary staff 137–138

natural teaching strategies 142
Neurofibromatosis 28
nonverbal/fluid reasoning 96
Noonan's syndrome 28

Obsessive-Compulsive Disorder 65
optimal outcomes 13–15
outcomes 13–16

parent interview 78–80
parent training 142
parental age 33
peer training package 142
Pennsylvania Association for Retarded Children (PARC) v. Commonwealth of Pennsylvania 10
Phenylketonuria 29
phonological processing 96
pivotal response training 142
postsecondary education 17–19
postsecondary employment 17–19

Prader-Willi syndrome 29
pregnancy factors: chemical exposures 35; folic acid 34; maternal antidepressant use 38; maternal health problems 34; maternal substance use 37
Preschool Language Scale, 5th edn (PLS-5) 90
preschool services 119
processing speed 96
prognosis 13–14
psychiatric comorbidities 62–67
psychological processes: assessment 95–97; patterns 97–98

Q.W. v Board of Education of Fayette County 118

rating scales 87–88: autism specific 87–88; broad band 88
reading skills 98–101: basic reading 98–99; concepts of print 98; hyperlexia 98–99; reading comprehension 99–100
record review 81
regression 12
Rehabilitation Act (Section 504) 10, 126–127: relationship to IDEA 116–117, 126
repetitive, restricted patterns of behavior 5–6
Response to Intervention 121–126: effectiveness for ASD 125; interventions 122; presenting problems 121
results: family reaction 135–136; sharing with parents 129–130; SPIKE model 130; written reports 136–137; *see also* Cultural differences; Monteiro triangle
Rett's syndrome 28

Scales of Independent Behavior, Revised (SIB-R) 86
schedules 142
schizophrenia 66–67
screening for autism 78
Screening Tool for Autism in Two Year Olds (STAT) 76
scripting 142
Section 504 *see* Rehabilitation Act

seizure disorders 58
self-management 142
Significant Developmental Delay
    special education eligibility 119;
    relation to ASD eligibility
sleep 67–68
SMART format 140
social Communication 3:
    milestones 4
Social Communication
    Questionnaire 87
Social Responsiveness Scale, 2nd edn
    (SRS-2) 87
Social Skills package 142
speech assessment 89
SPIKE model 130
Stanford-Binet Intelligence Scales, 5th
    edn (SB-V) 83, 96,
story-based intervention 142

Test of Auditory Processing, 4th edn
    (TAPS-4) 97
Test of Pragmatic Language, 2nd edn
    (TOPL-2) 90
transition planning 16–19, 119, 133,
    142–143
Tuberous sclerosis 28

Universal Nonverbal Intelligence Test,
    2nd edn (UNIT-2) 83

vaccination 35–37
verbal/crystallized reasoning 96
Vineland Adaptive Behavior Scales,
    3rd edn (VABS-3) 86
visual impairment 59–60
visual schedules 64, 137
visual–spatial–orthographic
    processing 96

Wechsler Individual Achievement
    Test, 3rd edn (WIAT-III) 95
Wechsler Intelligence Scale for
    Children, 5th edn (WISV-5)
    83, 96
Wechsler Preschool and Primary
    Scales of Intelligence, 4th edn
    (WPPSI-IV) 82
William's syndrome 28
Woodcock Johnson IV Tests of
    Achievement 95
Woodcock Johnson Test of Cognitive
    Abilities 83, 96
working memory 96
written expression skills 103–105

Printed in the United States
by Baker & Taylor Publisher Services